Contents

Society as **I H**ave Found **I**t

The Cuisine, Culture and Fashions of Europe and North America in the 19th Century, by a Man who Toured the Era's Finest Events and State Functions

By Ward McAllister

Published by Pantianos Classics

ISBN-13: 978-1-78987-175-3

First published in 1890

"This book is intended to be miscellaneous, with a noble disdain of regularity."

—*Obiter Dicta.*

"How then does a man, be he good or bad, big or little, make his Memoirs interesting? To say that the one thing needful is individuality, is not quite enough. To have an individuality is no sort of distinction, but to be able to make it felt in writing is not only distinction, but under favorable circumstances, immortality."

—*The Same.*

Author's Note

One who reads this book through will have as rough a mental journey as his physical nature would undergo in riding over a corduroy road in an old stage-coach. It makes no pretension to either scholarship or elegant diction.

W. McA.

Chapter One

In 1820 my mother, a beautiful girl of eighteen years, was introduced into New York society by her sister, Mrs. Samuel Ward, the wife of Samuel Ward, the banker, of the firm of Prime, Ward & King. She was a great belle in the days when Robert and Richard Ray and Prescott Hall were of the *jeunesse dorée* of this city. In my opinion, she was the most beautiful, Murillo-like woman I have ever seen, and she was as good as she was beautiful;—an angel in works of charity and sympathy for her race. Charlotte Corday's picture in the Louvre is a picture of my mother. The likeness arose from the fact that her family were descended on the maternal side from the Corday family of France. This also accounts for all my family being, from time immemorial, good Democrats. No one was too humble to be received and cared for and sympathized with by my mother. Her pastime was by the bedside of hospital patients, and in the schoolroom of her children. She followed the precepts of her mother's great-grandfather, the Rev. Gabriel Marion (grandfather of Gen. Francis Marion) as expressed in his will to the following effect: "As to the poor, I have always treated them as my brethren. My dear family will, I know, follow my example." It also contained this item: "I give her, my wife, my new carriage and horses, that she may visit her friends in comfort." This ancestor came from Rochelle in a large ship chartered for the Carolinas by several wealthy Huguenot families. The Hugers and Trapiers and others came over in the same ship. He did not leave France empty-handed, for on his arrival in Carolina he bought a plantation on Goose Creek, near Charleston, where he was buried.

While a belle in this city her admirers were legion, until a young Georgian, in the person of my father, stepped in, and secured the prize and took her off to Savannah. He was fresh from Princeton College, cut short in his college career by a large fire in Savannah (his native city), which burnt it down, destroying my grandfather's city property. The old gentleman, when the fire occurred, refused to leave his residence (now the Pulaski Hotel), and was taken forcibly from the burning building in his chair. He then owned the valuable business portion of the city, and at once went to work to rebuild. His relatives would not assist him, and so he sent for his only son, then at college, and got him to indorse all his notes, and in this way secured from the banks the money he wanted for building purposes. He undertook too much, and my father bore for one-third of his life a burden of debt then incurred. Nothing daunted, he went to work at the bar and commenced life with his beautiful, young Northern wife.

At that time, there was a great prejudice against Northern people. My father's mother never forgave my mother for being a Northern woman, and when she died, though she knew her son was weighed down with his father's debts, insisted on his freeing all the negroes she owned and left him by will, enjoining him to do this as her last dying request. It is needless to say that he did it, and not only this, but became the guardian of those people and helped and cared for them so long as he lived. Being repeatedly Mayor of the City of Savannah, he was able to protect them, and so devoted were the whole colored population to him, that one Andrew Marshall, the clergyman of the largest colored church in the city of Savannah, offered up prayers for him on every Sunday, as is done in our Episcopal church for the President of the United States. Blest with five sons and one daughter, struggling to maintain them by his practice at the bar, this best of fathers sent his family North every summer, with one or two exceptions, to Newport, R. I., which at that time was really a Southern colony.

It was the fashion then at Newport to lease for the summer a farmer's house on the Island, and not live in the town. Well do I remember, with my Uncle Sam Ward and Dr. Francis, of New York, and my father, building bonfires on Paradise Rocks on the Fourth of July and flying kites from Purgatory. The first relief to this hard-worked man was sending his oldest son to West Point, where, I will here add, he did the family great credit by becoming, being, and dying a noble soldier and Christian. Fighting in both armies, one may say, though I believe he was in active service only in the Mexican War, having graduated second in his class at West Point and entered the Ordnance Corps; so in place of fighting, he was making arms, casting cannon, etc. His pride lay in the fact that he was a soldier. His last request was that the Secretary of War should grant permission for his remains to be buried at West Point, which request was granted. My second brother, Hall, grew up with the poet Milton always under his arm. He was a great student. At the little village of Springfield, Georgia, where my family had a country house, and where we occasionally passed the summer in the piney woods, I remember as a boy of fifteen years of age, reading the Declaration of Independence on the Fourth of July from the pulpit of the village church to the descendants of the old Salzburghers, who came over soon after Oglethorpe, and it was before an audience of these piney woods farmers, that, with this brother, at a meeting of our Debating Society in this village, I discussed the question, "Which is the stronger passion, Love or Ambition," he advocating Ambition, I Love. I well remember going for him, as follows: "If his motto be that of Hercules the Invincible, I assume for mine that of his opponent, Venus the Victorious. With my sling and stone I will enter this unequal combat and thus hope to slay the great Goliath." The twelve good and true men who heard the discussion decided in my favor. To the end of his days this brother of mine was guided and governed by this self-same ambition; it made him what he became, a great lawyer, the lawyer of the Pacific coast; his boast to me being that he had saved seventeen lives, never having lost a murder case. I let ambition go, and through life and to the present moment swear by my goddess Venus. This brother, after entering the Georgia bar, started for a trip around the world.

8

On reaching San Francisco he heard of the discovery of gold, and Commodore Jones, then in command of our Pacific Squadron, urged him to prosecute some sailors who had thrown an officer overboard and deserted, and it was this which caused him to settle down there to the practice of law.

Chapter Two - Law and Housekeeping

I myself soon left Savannah for New York after Hall's departure, residing there in Tenth Street with an old maiden lady, my relative and godmother, whom I always felt would endow me with all her worldly goods, but who, I regret to say, preferred the Presbyterian church and the Georgia Historical Society to myself, for between them she divided a million. At that time Tenth Street was a fashionable street; our house was a comfortable, ordinary one, but my ancient relative considered it a palace, so that all her visitors were taken from garret to cellar to view it. Occupying the front room in the third story, as I would hear these visitors making for my room, I often had to scramble into the bath-room or under the bed, to hide myself. Having a large fortune, my relative, whom I called Aunt (but who was really only my father's cousin), was saving to meanness; her plantations in the South furnished our table; turkeys came on in barrels. "It was turkey hot and turkey cold, turkey tender, and turkey tough, until at grace one would exclaim, 'I thank ye, Lord, we've had enough.'" As the supposed heir of my saving godmother, the portals of New York society were easily open to me, and I well remember my first fancy ball, given by Mrs. John C. Stevens in her residence in College Place. A company of soldiers were called in to drill on the waxed floors to perfect them for dancing. A legacy of a thousand dollars paid me by the New York Life Insurance and Trust Company I expended in a fancy dress, which I flattered myself was the handsomest and richest at the ball. I danced the cotillion with a nun, a strange costume for her to appear in, as "I wont be a nun" was engraved on every expression of her face. She was at that day one of the brightest and most charming young women in this city, and had a power of fascination rarely equaled.

The next great social event that I recall was the great fancy ball given by the Schermerhorns in their house on the corner of Great Jones Street and Lafayette Place. All the guests were asked to appear in the costume of the period of Louis XV. The house itself was furnished and decorated in that style for this occasion. No pains or expense were spared. It was intended to be the greatest *affaire de luxe* New Yorkers had ever seen. The men, as well as the women, vied with each other in getting up as handsome costumes as were ever worn at that luxurious Court. The lace and diamonds on the women astonished society. All the servants of the house wore costumes, correct copies of those worn at that period. The men in tights and silk stockings, for the first time in their lives, became jealous of each other's calves, and in one instance, a friend of mine, on gazing at the superb development in this line of a guest, doubted nature's having bestowed such generous gifts on him; so, to satisfy himself, he pricked his neighbor's calf with his sword, actually drawing blood, but the possessor of the fine limbs never winced; later on he expressed forcibly his opinion of the assault. By not wincing the impression that he had aided nature was confirmed.

These two balls were the greatest social events that had ever occurred in this city. Even then subscription balls were the fashion. One of the most brilliant was given at Delmonico's on the corner of Beaver and William streets (the old building in which the ball was given is now being torn down). Saracco's dancing-rooms were then much resorted to. They became the rage, and every one was seized with a desire to perfect himself in dancing.

Disgusted with book-keeping, I resolved to study law, and knowing that I could not do much studying whilst flirting and going to balls and dinners, I went South to my native city, took up the second volume of Blackstone, committed it to memory, passed an examination, and was admitted to the bar by one of our ex-ministers to Austria, then a judge.

Blackstone did not wholly absorb all my time that winter. I exercised my memory in the morning and indulged my imagination of an afternoon, breathing soft words to lovely Southern maidens, in the piney groves which surround that charming city. From time immemorial they had always given these on Valentine's Eve a Valentine party. I was tempted to go to the one given that year. And as I entered the house a basketful of sealed envelopes was handed me, one of which I took; on breaking the seal, I found on the card the name of a brilliant, charming young woman, whom I then had a right to claim as my partner for the evening, but to whom I must bend the knee, and express interest and devotion to her in a species of poetical rhapsody. As all the young men were to go through the same ordeal, it was less embarrassing. From the time of entering the ball-room until the late hour at which supper was served, the guests in the crowded rooms were laughing over the sight of each young man dropping on one knee before his partner and presenting her with a bouquet of flowers, and in low and tender words pouring out his soul in poetry. When it came my turn, I secured a cushion and down I went, the young woman laughing immoderately; but I, not in the least perturbed, grasping my bouquet of flowers with one hand and placing my other hand over my heart, looking into the depths of her lovely eyes, addressed to her these words:

"These flowers, dear lady, unto thee I bring,
With hopes as timid as the dawning spring,
Which oft repelled by many a chilling blast
Still trusts its offerings may succeed at last.

Receive thou, emblem of the rosy spring,
Charmer of life, of every earthly thing,

10

These flowers, which lovely as the tints of morn
Yet ne'er can hope thy beauty to adorn.

Oh, may they plead for one who never knew
Perfection's image till he met with you;
Oh, may their fragrance to thy heart convey
How much he would, but does not dare to say."

In the mean time, while I was dancing and reciting poetry to beautiful women, my generous brother was rapidly making money at the bar in San Francisco, and urging my father and me to leave Georgia and go to him, writing that he was making more money in two months' practice than my father received in a year. This to my conservative parent seemed incredible; he shook his head, saying to me, "It is hard for an old tree to take root in a new soil." His friends of the Savannah bar ridiculed his entertaining the notion of leaving Georgia, where his father had been a Judge of the Superior Court of that State; he himself had been United States District Attorney, for years had presided over the Georgia Senate, had been nominated for Governor of the State, and for a lifetime had been at the head of the Georgia bar. Always a Union man, opposing Nullification, he was beloved by the people of his State, and his law practice was then most lucrative. The idea of his pulling up stakes and going to the outposts of civilization seemed absurd. He would not entertain the thought; he laughed at my brother's Arabian Nights stories of his law firm in San Francisco making money at the rate of $100,000 a year. But just here, my father's purpose was suddenly shaken, by my brother's remitting to me a large amount of money in gold dust, and he, my father, being then paid five thousand dollars by the Bank of the State of Georgia for an argument made for them before the United States Supreme Court at Washington. My gold dust was tangible evidence of my brother's success, and as continual dropping wears away a stone, so by continual pleading I at last persuaded him to take me to California. Mournfully he sold our old homestead and sadly closed up his Savannah law office, and with me, on the 13th of May, 1850, left for San Francisco, where in two years he made a comfortable fortune, retired from practice and went to Europe. My brother Hall's motto was, "Ten millions or nothing." He made himself, to my certain knowledge, two comfortable fortunes. Grand speculations to double my father's fortune very soon made inroads in it, and the dear old gentleman to save a remnant returned to this country. As he expressed himself to me, "California must have a Circuit Judge of the United States. I will get our Democratic Congress to pass a bill to this effect, and will myself return to California as its United States Circuit Judge. I do not care to return to the practice of law when I reach San Francisco, where, I expect to find that, like the 'fruit of the Dead Sea,' my little competency will turn into ashes at the touch. Being on the Bench, I shall at least have a support"; all of which he carried out to the letter, and he died devoted to the people of the State of California.

Imagine me then, a well-fed man, with always an appreciative appetite,

11

learning, on my arrival in San Francisco, that eggs, without which I could not breakfast, cost $2 apiece, a fowl $8, a turkey $16. One week's mess bill for my breakfast and dinner alone was $225, and one visit to my doctor cost me $50. Gloom settled upon me, until my noble parent requested me to bring back to the office our first retainer (for I was then a member of my father and brother's law firm). It was $4000 in gold ounces. I put it in a bag and lugged it to the office, and as I laid them ounce by ounce on my father's desk, he danced a pirouette, for he was as jolly an old fellow as ever lived. I went to work at once in earnest; it struck me that in that country it was "root, pig, or die."

My first purchase was a desk, which combined the qualities of bed and desk. How well I remember the rats playing hide-and-seek over me at night, and over the large barrel of English Brown Stout that I invested in and placed in the entry to console myself with. After six months' hard work, I began to ease up, and feel rich. I built a small house for myself, the front entry 4 × 4, the back entry the same, one dining-room 12 × 14, and one bedroom, same dimensions. My furniture, just from Paris, was acajou and white and blue horsehair. My bed-quilt cost me $250; it was a lovely Chinese floss silk shawl. An Indian chief, calling to see me, found me in bed, and was so delighted with the blankets that he seized hold of them and exclaimed, "*Quanto pesos?*" (How much did they cost?)

My first row as a householder was with my neighbor, a Texan. I found my yard fence, if put up, would close up the windows and front door of his house. We had an interview. He, with strong adjectives, assured me that he would blow out my brains if I put up that fence. I asked him in reply, where he kept his private burying ground. All men then went armed day and night. For two years I slept with a revolver under my pillow. With a strong force of men the next day, I put up the fence, and the Texan moved out and sold his lot. As our firm was then making $100,000 a year, our senior partner, my father, asked me to entertain, for the firm, our distinguished European clients, as he himself had not the time to do so. His injunction to me was, "Be sure, my boy, that you always invite nice people." I had heard that my dear old father had on more than one occasion gotten off a witticism on me as follows: Being told how well his son kept house, he replied, "Yes, he keeps everything but the Ten Commandments," so I assured him if he would honor me with his presence I would have to meet him every respectable woman in the city, and I kept my word. Before we reached the turkey, my guests had so thoroughly dined that when it appeared, the handsomest woman in the room heaved a deep sigh and exclaimed, "Oh, that I might have some of it for lunch to-morrow!" Such dinners as I then gave, I have never seen surpassed anywhere. It is needless to say that my father was intensely gratified. We had, tempted by exaggerated accounts of the gold fields, French cooks who received $6000 a year as salary. The turkey, costly as it was at $16, always came on table with its feathered tail intact, and as eggs were so expensive, *omelette soufflée* was always the dish at dessert. Two years was the length of my stay in San Francisco.

On reaching New York in 1852, from California, I found great objection made to my return there as a married man, and gracefully yielded to circumstances. Though loath to give up my profession of the law, I was forced to make this sacrifice; so the moment I concluded to give up California and the legal profession, not wishing to be idle, I went to Washington and applied to the President for the position of Secretary of Legation in England. The Georgia, South Carolina, Virginia, and California delegations urged me for this appointment; Mr. Buchanan was going to England as Minister. He was a warm friend of my father's, and, when approached, expressed not only willingness but gratification at having the son of an old friend as his Secretary of Legation, and I was to have had the position. But just at this time, my father, who had returned from Europe, wished to obtain from President Pierce the appointment of Circuit Judge of the United States for the State of California. He came to me and stated the case as follows: "My boy," he said, "the President says he cannot give two appointments to one family. If you go to England as Buchanan's Secretary, President Pierce cannot make me Circuit Judge of California." "Enough said," I replied, "I yield with pleasure. I will go abroad, but not in the diplomatic service." Passing the winter in Washington, I soon learned how to ingratiate myself with the law-makers of our country. Good dinners and wine were always effective. And as I had the friendship of the California, New York and Southern delegations, I was dining out all the time, invited by one man or other who had an axe to grind. On these occasions, there was always a room prepared to receive a guest who had indulged too freely in strong waters. Men then drank in good earnest, a striking contrast to the days in which we now live, when really, at dinner, people only taste wine, but do not drink it. I was then placed on the Committee of Management for the Inaugural Ball, and did good service and learned much from my Washington winter.

An amusing incident I must here relate. Quietly breakfasting and chatting with a beautiful woman, then a bride, who had lived for years in Washington as a widow, she asked me if I was going to Corcoran's ball that evening, and on my replying, "Yes, of course I was," she requested me to accompany her husband and self, which I did. On entering Mr. Corcoran's ball room with her on my arm, I noticed that the old gentleman bowed very stiffly to us; however, I paid no attention to this and went on dancing, and escorting through the rooms my fair partner, from whom I had no sooner been separated than my host slapped me on the shoulder with, "My dear young man, I know you did not know it, but the lady you have just had on your arm is not only not a guest of mine, but this morning I positively refused to send her an invitation to this ball." Fortunately I had brought letters to this distinguished man, so seeing my annoyance, he patted me on the shoulder and said, "My boy, this is not an unusual occurrence in this city; but let it be a warning to you to take care hereafter whom you bring to a friend's house"

Chapter Three – Introduction to London Sports

After my marriage I took up my residence in Newport, buying a farm on Narragansett Bay and turning farmer in good earnest. I planted out 10,000 trees on that farm and then went to Europe to let them grow, expecting a forest on my return, but I found only one of them struggling for existence three years later. In London, I met a Californian, in with all the sporting world, on intimate terms with the champion prize-fighter of England, the Queen's pages, Tattersall's and others. He suggested that if I would defray the expense, he would show me London as no American had ever seen it. Agreeing to do this, I was taken to a swell tailor in Regent Street, to put me, as he expressed it, "in proper rig." My first introduction to London life was dining out in the suburbs to see a dog-fight, and sup at a Regent Street dry-goods merchant's residence. I was introduced as an American landed proprietor. Mine host, I was told, spent twelve thousand pounds, i.e. $60,000 a year, on his establishment. He was an enthusiast in his way, an old sport. The women whom I was invited to meet looked like six-footers; the hall of the house and the sitting-rooms were filled with stuffed bull-terriers, prize dogs, that had done good service. We walked through beautifully laid-out grounds to a miniature ornamental villa which contained a rat pit, and there we saw a contest between what seemed to me a myriad of rats and a bull-terrier. The latter's work was expeditious. We surrounded the pit, each one with his watch in hand timing the dog's work, which he easily accomplished in the allotted time, killing all the rats, which called forth great applause. From this pit we went to another, where we saw the drawing of the badger, a very amusing sight. There was a long narrow box with a trap-door, by which the badger was shut in; up went the door, in went the terrier; he seized the badger by the ear and pulled him out of his box and around the pit, the badger held back with all his might; should the dog fail to catch the badger by the ear, the badger would kill him. Again, we assembled around a third pit, to see a dog-fight, and saw fight after fight between these bull-terriers, to me a disgusting sight, but the women shouted with delight, and kept incessantly calling "Time, sir; time, sir!" Large bets were made on the result. At midnight we went to supper. I sat next to the champion prize-fighter of England, who informed me that a countryman of mine had died in his arms after a prize-fight. Such drinking I never saw before or since; the host, calling for bumper after bumper, insisted on every one draining his glass. I skillfully threw my wine under the table. The host and all the company were soon intoxicated. The footmen in green and gold liveries never cracked a smile. The master, after a bumper, would fall forward on the table, smashing everything. His butler picked him up and replaced him in his chair. This was kept up until 3 A.M., when with pleasure I slipped out and was off in my hansom for London.

My visit to Windsor Castle, dining at the village inn with Her Majesty's *chef*, and the keeper of her jewel room, was interesting. I saw the old, tall door-keeper, with his long staff, sitting at the door of the servants' hall. I saw Her Majesty's kitchen and the roasts for all living in the castle,—at least twenty separate pieces turning on a spit. Then I examined a large, hot, steel table on which any cooked article being placed would stay hot as long as it remained there. The *chef* told me a German prince, when informed of its price, said it would take all his yearly revenue to pay for it. Then I saw Her Majesty's jewel room; the walls wainscoted, as it were, with gold plates; the large gold bowl, which looks like a small bath-tub, from which the Prince of Wales was baptized, stood in the dining-room. I saw Prince Albert and the Prince of Wales that morning shooting pheasants, alongside of the Windsor Long Walk, and stood within a few yards of them. I feel sure we ate, that day, at the inn, the pheasants that had been shot by Prince Albert. I visited Her Majesty's model farm, and found that all the flax-seed cake for the cattle was imported from America. The simple cognomen, American Landed Proprietor, was "open sesame" to me everywhere, accompanied as I was by one of her Majesty's pages. In London, of an evening, we went to Evans's, a sort of public hall where one took beer and listened to comic songs. Jubber, a wine merchant, kept the hotel where I lodged. As a celebrated London physician was dining with me, I asked for the palest and most delicate sherry to be found in London, regardless of cost, to be served that day, at my dinner. He looked at me and smiled, seeing I was quite a young man, saying, "If I give it to you, you will not drink it." "Send me the sherry," I replied, "and you will see." The result was I got a delicious Montilla sherry and sent a butt of it to America. This was my first acquaintance with Montilla sherry, the most delicate wine that I know of, to be served from soup to dessert.

Before getting through with my sporting friend, after paying all his expenses and remunerating him liberally for his services, as I was about to cross the Channel, he came up to me and said, "Mc, I want you to lend me some money." I saw by his face he was in earnest, and thought that he was about to make a demand for a large amount. So, equally serious, I replied, "It is out of the question, my dear fellow; I am here in a strange country with my family and have no money to lend." He roared, "Why, all I wanted was a shilling to pay for the *Times*," which made me feel very sheepish. That was the last I saw of him. When two years later I returned to London, I found he had conscientiously paid no bills, and, strange to relate, his hotel keeper and tailors seemed fully compensated for the food and raiment they had furnished him, by his sending them a few valueless colored plates of sporting scenes in this country.

Chapter Four – A Winter in Italy

I landed in France, not knowing how to speak the language, and only remembering a few French words learned in childhood. It was the year of the

Paris Exposition of 1857; all the hotels were full. The Meurice Hotel people sent me off to a neighboring house, where we lodged in the ninth story. I saw the baptism of the Prince Imperial, and on that occasion, and later on in Rome, at the Carnival, saw the handsomest women I had yet seen in Europe. We then made for Florence, and there, getting a most captivating little apartment, on the Arno, kept house, and if it had not been for the terrible and incessant winds called the *tramontana* would probably have passed our days there. I had the most admirable cook, and had never lived as well. Then the economy of the thing; it cost nothing to live. I paid the fellow twenty-four pauls ($2.40) a day. For this sum he gave us breakfast and exquisite dinners. For each extra guest, at dinner, I paid a few pauls; if I gave a dinner party he hired for me as handsome a service of silver plate as I have ever seen. His whole kitchen seemed to consist of half a dozen pots and pans, and everything was cooked by charcoal.

His manner of roasting a turkey was indeed novel; he placed his bird on a spit, put it in an iron pot, covered it with hot coals top and bottom, and then kept turning the spit incessantly and basting the bird. Such a perfect roast I have never before or since eaten. I shall speak later on of the Newport turkey and the Southern barnyard-fed turkey, but they are not a circumstance to the Florentine walnut-fed turkey. In Florence, at the markets, all turkeys and fowls were cut up and sold, not as a whole, but piece by piece. For instance, you saw on the marble slabs the breasts of chickens, the wings of chickens, the legs of chickens; the same with turkeys. To get an entire bird, you had to order him ahead, so that a few days before Christmas, as we came home from our drive, we found a superb turkey strutting through the drawing-room, the largest creature I had ever seen, weighing twenty-five pounds. When he was served, the walnuts he had eaten could be seen all over his back in large, round yellow spots of fat. As he came on the table, he was indeed a sight to behold; the skin, as it were, mahogany color and crisp, his flesh partaking of the flavor of the walnut, would have satisfied Lucullus.

At that period I worshipped doctors; my theory then was that you owed your existence to them, that they kept you in the world, and not to have a doctor within call was to place yourself in danger of immediate and sudden death; so the first man I cultivated in Florence was the English doctor. He came to see me every day; it was indeed a luxury; his fee was two dollars. We became great friends, and as he was the Court physician, he got me invitations to all the balls. The Grand Duke of Tuscany, then the richest sovereign in Europe, gave a ball every fortnight at the Pitti Palace. It was said that the Italians lived on chestnuts and air between these suppers, and, like the bear, laid in such a supply of food at them as comfortably to carry them through from one entertainment to the other. Certainly such feasting I had never before seen. The number of rooms thrown open really confused one, it was hard not to lose one's way. All the guests were assembled, and grouped in the form of a circle, in the largest of these salons, when the grand ducal party entered. The minister of each foreign country stood at the head of his little band of countrymen and countrywomen who were to be presented. The Grand Duke, Archduke, and suite passed from group to group. The presentation over, the ball began in earnest. All waited until the Archduke started in the dance, and as he waltzed by you, you followed. When he stopped dancing, all stopped.

I remember, at one of these balls, dancing with an American girl, a strikingly handsome woman, a great Stonington belle. As we waltzed by the King of Bavaria, I felt a hand placed on my shoulder, and a voice exclaimed, "*Mais, Monsieur, c'est le roi*"; I stopped at once, and hastily inquired of my fair partner, "What is it?" She replied, "I did it, I was determined to do it. As I passed the King I punched him in the ribs with my elbow. Now I am satisfied." I rushed up to the King and Grand Chamberlain, saying, "*Mille pardons, mille pardons*," and the affair passed over, but I soon disposed of the young woman and never "attempted her again." The diamonds the women wore amazed me. You see nothing in this country like the tiaras of diamonds I saw at this ball; tiara after tiara, the whole head blazing with diamonds, and yet there was but little beauty.

It was here that I first learned what a ball supper should be, and what were the proper mural decorations for a ball-room and the halls opening into it. The supper system was perfect. In one salon, large tables for coffee, tea, chocolate, and cakes. In another, tables covered simply with ices and other light refreshments, *foie gras*, sandwiches, etc. In the grand supper room, the whole of the wall of one side of the room, from floor almost to ceiling, was covered with shelves, on which every imaginable dish was placed, hot and cold. The table in front of these shelves was lined with servants in livery, and simply loaded with empty plates and napkins to serve the supper on. The favorite and most prized dishes at all these suppers was cold sturgeon (a fish we never eat), and the most prized fruit the hot-house pineapple, with all its leaves, and to the eye seemingly growing. Opposite the supper table, in another part of the room, the wines were served, all by themselves, and there was, it appears to me, every wine grown in any quarter of the globe. Everything was abundant and lavish, and the whole affair was most imposing.

That winter the Archduke of Tuscany married one of the princesses of Bavaria, and the Austrian Minister gave them a ball, which I attended. The effect produced in approaching his palace, all the streets illuminated by immense flaring torches attached to the house, was grand. The ball-room was superb. From the ceiling hung, not one or two, but literally fifty or more chandeliers of glass, with long prisms dangling from them. The women were not handsome, but what most struck me was the freshness of their toilets. They all looked new, as if made for the occasion; not so elaborate, but so fresh and light and delicate. I noticed that the royal party supped in a room by themselves, always attended by their host.

As I was strolling through the rooms, my host, the Austrian Minister, approached me and said, "I see I have another American as a guest to-night, and he is decorated. Will you kindly tell me what his decoration is?" "I really do not know," I replied; "I will present myself to him and ask."

We approached my countryman together, and, after a few words, the minister most courteously put the question to him. He drew himself up and said, "Sir, my country is a Republic; if it had been a Monarchy, I would have been the Duke of Pennsylvania. The Order I wear is that of The Cincinnati." The minister, deeply impressed, withdrew, and I intensely enjoyed the little scene.

After the great works of art, what most impressed me in Florence were the immense, orderly crowds seen on all public occasions, a living mass of humanity, as far as the eye could see. No jostling or shoving, but human beings filling up every inch of space between the carriage wheels, as our horses, on a walk, dragged our carriage through them.

The most charming spot on earth for the last of winter and the spring months is the city of Rome. We went there under most favorable circumstances. A kind friend had leased an apartment for us in the Via Gregoriana, and we found Rome full of the *crême de la crême* of New York society. In Nazzari we had another Delmonico, and we kept dining and wining each other daily. Here I made intimacies that have lasted me through life. I followed the hounds on the Campagna, and was amused at the nonchalance of the young Italian swells as they would attempt a high Campagna fence, tumble off invariably, remount, and go at it again. They were a handsome set of men, as plucky as they were handsome. I myself found "discretion the better part of valor," and would quietly take to the road when I met a formidable jump, but I lived on horseback and enjoyed every hour. Though carrying letters to our American Minister, then resident at Rome, I gave his legation a wide berth, as I had heard that our distinguished Representative was in the habit of inviting Italians to meet Italians and Americans to meet only Americans at his house; when asked his reason for this, he replied: "I have the greatest admiration for my countrymen: they are enterprising, money getting, in fact, a wonderful nation, but there is not a gentleman among them." Hearing this, I resolved he should get no chance to meet me and pass on my merits.

Several of our handsomest New York women were then having their busts sculptured in marble; as you saw them first in the clay you found them more attractive. Gibson for the first time colored his Venus; it added warmth to it, and I thought improved it.

The blessing of the multitude by the Pope from the balcony of St. Peter's, under a canopy, with the emblematic peacock feathers held on either side of him, the illumination of St. Peter's, and the fireworks at Easter were most impressive. But I shall attempt no description of Rome. Nowhere in the world can you see such a display.

Chapter Five – Germany and the Alps

We passed our summer at Baden-Baden and literally lived there in the open air. Opposite to my apartment, Prince Furstenburg of Vienna had his hotel: from him and his suite I learned how to spend the summer months. At early dawn they were out in the saddle for a canter; at ten they went for a drive down the Allée Lichtenthal and through shady woods, nowhere seen as at Baden-Baden. They would stop and breakfast in the open air at twelve noon, again drive in the afternoon, and dine at the Kursaal at six. They kept at least twenty-five horses. We dined daily within a table or two of the then Prince of Prussia, afterwards the Emperor William, whom I soon discovered was no judge of wine, as I drank the best and he was evidently indifferent to it. When you see a man sip his wine and linger over it, that evidences his appreciation of it; but when you see him gulp it down, as the Prince did his, you see that he is no connoisseur. But I must say here, I had an intense admiration for him. His habit of walking two hours under the trees of the Allée Lichtenthal was also mine, and it was with pleasure I bowed most respectfully to him day by day.

Being anxious to cross every Alpine pass, I found a distinguished physician who lived at Pau, France, on account of his health, and had there the practice of the place during the winter months, and who was, necessarily, idle in summer, as Pau was then deserted. Still believing in doctors, I engaged him to travel with me for two months as my physician. I agreed to give him a bottle of 1848 Latour for his dinner daily, pay his expenses, and to give him a medical fee such as I saw fit at the end of our trip. He was indeed a man among men. All I can say is that when we parted and I handed him his fee, the tears came into his eyes; he grasped my hands, swearing eternal friendship. This doctor made a new man of me. "Throw physic to the dogs," was his motto; "you will never die: you will in the end have to be shot to get you out of the world; air and exercise is all you want: eat slowly and do not deluge yourself with water at dinner." Of water he had a holy horror. "Drink what good wine you wish and let water alone." As I had the luxury of a private physician, a friend from Louisiana suggested joining my party with his two young daughters. My Irish doctor was the most sensitive of men. One day I found he could eat no breakfast. I sympathized with him and asked him the cause. He replied, "My dear boy, the habits of your American women. I came down to the breakfast room this morning and there I found the oldest of the Judge's daughters with her back hair down and the younger one combing it. This settled me." I assured him this was not the national custom with American women. The young woman was simply trying to captivate him by her lovely, long, flowing tresses. The doctor was a character. On another occasion a Frenchman lighted a cigar in our railway compartment. The Doctor detested cigar smoke, and as there was a large sign in the car, in French, forbidding smoking, he touched the Frenchman and pointed to the sign. The Frenchman simply smiled blandly. The train stopping, the conductor opened our door, when the Frenchman quietly slipped two francs into his hands, saying in French, "Of course I can smoke here, that sign is obsolete, is it not?" The conductor replied, "Oh, yes," and on we went. My Irishman got up and commenced taking his coat off. "What are you going to do?" exclaimed the Frenchman. "Why, throw you out of that window if you do not at once throw that cigar away." There was no mistaking the Doctor's meaning, so the cigar went out and the Frenchman staid in.

My traveling Louisiana friend had a charming way of suggesting each morning, as we paid our hotel bills, that we should toss up a five-franc piece and decide, by heads and tails, who was to pay the bill. I did this once or twice, when I found, as he always won and I lost, it was a losing business for me; but on another occasion was forced into the plan. To ascend the mountain at Lugano, three wretched beasts were brought us by the Italian boys to mount for the ascent. The Judge insisted on tossing up a five-franc piece for choice of animals. I was compelled to give in and accede to his suggestion, and by great good luck won first choice. My friend, the Judge, forbade the Doctor advising me as to the animal I should take, as he knew him to be a good judge of horses. There was a feeble, worthless horse that literally could carry no one; his back all raw; a vicious mule who bit and kicked, and a stone blind pony that would not go. With my experience of mules in the South, knowing what sure-footed creatures they were, I chose the mule, had him blindfolded, mounted him, and off I went. After waiting an hour on the summit, the Judge appeared, coat and hat gone, and swearing terribly that he would prosecute the canton for his treatment, and horsewhip the Italian boys. He had let the horse go, and footed it. I soon slipped away on my mule, letting the irate Louisianian and the Irishman settle it, on top of the mountain, how they were to have satisfaction out of the government for permitting such beasts to be imposed upon travelers. I was two-thirds down the mountain when I looked behind me and heard the most terrible shouts, and saw the Irishman clinging to the pony, over whom he had lost all control, and the Judge hanging on by the pony's tail, all coming down at a terrific pace. The pony was at first gentle, but it appears would not go beyond a walk. The Judge hung on to his tail to guide himself down the mountain, and finding he would not go fast enough to suit them, he assured the Irishman he would fix him, and immediately stuck his penknife into the beast's tail. "Fix him," he did, for the creature was so terrified he dashed off at a break-neck pace, and the Judge, not wishing to be left alone on the mountain, had to hang on by the tail and be dragged along at lightning speed. These beasts alone knew the way down; once parted from them, they were lost, for the Italian boys who had furnished them had long since fled from the Judge's wrath. The Judge and the Doctor forbade my paying the hotel bill, and I had to do it surreptitiously.

My doctor (who was a victim to rheumatism) called my attention to the fact that on the summit of every Alpine pass we crossed, after all other vegetation ceased, the aconite plant grew, showing nature had provided there a remedy for the disease which the severity of the climate developed in man. My Irish friend, living far from the sea, had a passion for all fish but pike, which he detested, and which was daily served to us wherever we went; finally, reaching Berlin, he insisted on having sea fish. It was promised us, but, lo and behold! when dinner was served, in came the pike, with the apology that no other fish could then be had in the city. After dinner we went to the opera, and there, in the ballet (superbly done as it was), were at least one hundred pike dancing on the stage, which so upset my friend that he seized his hat in a rage and left the house.

Chapter Six – Winter in Pau

After you have been a little while in Europe you are seized with a desire to have a house of your own, to enjoy home comforts. Your loss of individuality comes over you. In Paris you feel particularly lost, and as this feeling increased on me I resolved to go to Pau, take a house, and winter there. The Duchess of Hamilton had abandoned the idea of passing the winter in Pau, so that many lovely residences were seeking tenants. For eight hundred dollars a year I hired a beautiful villa, looking on the Pyrénées, directly opposite the *Pic du Midi d'Ossau*, with lovely grounds filled with camelia bushes, and I then felt that I had all a man could desire,—a perfect home made to one's hand, a climate where the wind never blows hard enough, even in winter, to stir a leaf on the trees, the best cooks in the world, and where people appeared to live but to eat well and sleep. A country of beautiful women; the peasantry a mixture of Spanish and French blood; the climate so soft and genial as to take away all harshness or roughness from their faces—rich Titian-like women, with fine coloring and superb figures—what more could man desire? I was, I may say, a pioneer American there.

A member of a distinguished New York family, who had been our Secretary of Legation at Madrid, had preceded me; he had a lovely English wife, was the master of the hounds, and gave me a cordial reception. I lived there two winters, with a luxury I have never since enjoyed, and literally for nothing, comparing one's expenses there to living in New York. The desire to entertain took possession of me and I gratified it; such dinners and such wines! I ran down to Bordeaux, made friends with all the wine fraternity there, tasted and criticised, and wormed myself into the good graces of the owners of those enormous Bordeaux *caves*, learned there for the first time what claret was, and how impossible it was to drink out of Bordeaux, what a Bordeaux connoisseur would call a perfect wine. There I learned how to give dinners;

to esteem and value the *Coq de Bruyère* of the Pyrénées and the *Pie de Mars* (squab Magpie).

Pau was filled with sick English people. I was one of the few sound men physically in the place. I dashed into society with a vim. My Louisiana friend, the Judge, followed me there, and I had my hands full in establishing him socially. Shrewd, and immensely clever, he came to me one day and said, "My friend, I am going to make a name for myself in this place; wait and you will see." Some little distance from Pau, there was a large tract of worthless land, utterly valueless, called *Les Landes*. Shepherds on stilts tended a few sheep on it. The judge at once had an interview with the Prêfet of the Basses Pyrénées (an officer similar to the governor of one of our States), and assured him of the feasibility of reclaiming all this land and making fine cotton fields of it. This scheme, wonderful to relate, was seized upon with avidity by the Prêfet, and my friend, the Judge, was asked to submit his views. This was all he wanted. Of course he never perfected his plans for such work. The Prêfet, however, was at once his friend and admirer, and he was made the distinguished and sought-after stranger of that winter. He then came to me to get up a dinner for him, to be given to his newly acquired friend, which he charged me to make the most brilliant and superb dinner ever given in that place. I well remember his order to the florist; "Furnish me for my table such a display of flowers as you would provide for your Emperor; spare no expense." I telegraphed to Paris and exhausted all my resources to give him what he wished. When his guests were all assembled in his *salon*, my friend could not remember who was to take in who to dinner; so with great coolness he walked over to me, and to distract the attention of his assembled guests, said, in a loud voice, "Your horses, I am told, have run away, upset your carriage, and killed the coachman." Instantly the French people sprang up, exclaiming, "What! what is it! is it possible!" while the Judge, in a low voice, whispered, "Tell me quick who is to take in Madame J., and who goes in with Count B.?" I told him, when he quietly said, "All made up, my boy, let them believe it." The dinner was a success, such a success that I resolved to give a ball myself on the arrival from Paris of one of our New York merchant princes, to whom I was much indebted.

The French papers gave a glowing account of this ball, and I was fairly launched into the French society of the Basses Pyrénées. It is hard to convince an old business man, who has had large experience and amassed a fortune, that any one can do anything in his line better than himself. Therefore, when I gave my merchant prince exquisite Bordeaux wines that I knew were incomparable, and extolled them, he quietly replied:

"Why, my young friend, these wines are all from the house of Barton & Guestier. Now, you must know, that the house of Johnson can alone furnish what I class as the best clarets. I have for forty years been in correspondence with that house, and will guarantee to produce here in Pau, from them, clarets and sauternes better than any your house of Barton & Guestier can send you." I took him up at once, and the wager was a fine dinner of twenty covers.

All I had to do was to write the above statement to Mr. Guestier, who at once sent me his own butler to serve the wines, and sent with him a "Haut Brion" and a Chateau Latour of 1848. As he termed it, *mise en bouteille tout à fait speciale hors de ligne*, whose smoothness, bouquet, and flavor surpassed anything I had ever dreamt of tasting. My merchant prince with his Johnson wines was beaten out of sight, and so mortified was he that the day after the dinner he sent me as a present all the wines Johnson had sent him.

The hunt was then really the feature of Pau life, for those who could not follow in the saddle would, after attending the meet, take to the roads and see the best of the run. General Bosquet, returning then to Pau, his native city, was fêted by both French and English. He had so distinguished himself in the Crimean War that all regarded him as a great hero. The English particularly wanted to express their admiration of him, so they asked him to appear with his friends at the next Meet, and follow in the hunt, promising him rare sport and a good run after a bagged fox. To do him honor, the French, to a man, ordered new hunting suits, all of them turned out in "pink," and being in force made indeed a great show.

My Irish doctor was by my side, in great good humor, and a wicked twinkle in his eye. Turning to me he said:

"You will soon see some fun; not one of these Frenchmen can take that jump; it is a *rasper*. Not a man of them will clear that bank and ditch."

I smiled at this, and felt that to the end of time it would always be English against French. It was cruel; but men should not pretend to ride after hounds when they cannot take the jumps.

"Look at those chaps," he said, "in spotless pink; not a man among them who can jump a horse to any purpose."

They were the nobility of the Basses Pyrénées, a splendid, gallant set of fellows; all prepared "to do or die." The master of the hounds raised his hat, the fox was turned out of the bag; he was given ten minutes' law; then the huntsman with his pack dashed away, clearing both bank and ditch. It was the severest jump they could find in any part of that country, purposely chosen for that reason. My doctor's little Irish boy, a lad of sixteen years, went at it, and cleared it at a bound. I saw the master of the hunt (an American, a splendid looking fellow, superbly mounted, and a beautiful rider), with General Bosquet at his side, turn to the General (who was riding one of his horses), and shout:

"General, dash the spurs into her; lift her head a bit, and follow me."

The General did not hesitate; he plunged the spurs into the beast, dashed ahead, and cleared bank and ditch. All his friends followed him. Forward they went, but only for a few rods, when every horse, as if shot, came to a full stop, planted his forefeet in front of him, and neither whip nor spur could budge him. None would take the jump; every Frenchman's face became ashey pale, and I really felt sorry for them. Not a Frenchman, with the exception of the General, took that jump. After this, the mere mention of fox hunting would set the Frenchmen wild. It was cruel, but it was sport.

Moral: Men should not attempt to do what is not in them.

Passing two winters at Pau and the summers at Baden-Baden, keeping four horses at the former place, following the hounds at least once a week, giving all through the winter from one to two dinners a week, with an English housekeeper, and living as well as I could possibly live, with the cost of my ball included, I did not spend half the amount in living that I am compelled to in New York. The ball cost me but eight hundred dollars.

Chapter Seven – Home Again

Called home by the stupidity of an agent, who was unable to treat with my old friend, Commodore Vanderbilt, for an extension of his lease of our dock property, most unwillingly we left our dear old Pau, with all its charming associations, and returned to New York.

I have always had a great fondness for men older than myself. Always preferring to associate with my superiors than my inferiors in intellect, and hence when brought in contact with one of America's noblest and most cultivated men (withal, the then richest man in the United States, if not in the world), by his son-in-law, with whom I had formed a close intimacy abroad, I sought his society, and he, in turn, appeared at least to enjoy mine. Dining with him constantly, I suggested that he should dine with me; to which he readily assented. So I went to Cranston, my landlord of the New York Hotel, and put him to his trumps to give me a suitable dinner. His hotel was then crowded, and I had actually to take down a bedstead and improvise a dining-room. Cranston was one of those hotel-keepers who worked as much for glory as for money. He gave us simply a perfect dinner, and my dear old friend and his wife enjoyed it. I remember his saying to me, "My young friend, if you go on giving such dinners as these you need have no fear of planting yourself in this city." I here give the menu of this dinner:

CARTE DU DINER.

Les Huitres, salées.

———

Le Potage de Consommé de Volaille, à la Royale.

———

Le Basse rayée, grillée, Sauce Remoulade.

———

Les Pommes de Terre, à la Lyonnaise.

———

La Mayonnaise de Homard, decorée à la gélée.

———

Le Filet de Bœuf, piqué, rôti, aux champignons.

—

Les Cailles, truffées, à la Financière.
Les Côtelettes d'Agneau, à la Soubise.
Les Tomates, à l'Americaine.
Les Petits Pois, à la Française.

—

Canvas-back Ducks, roasted.
Le Celeri, au jus.

—

Les Huitres, grillées, à la Ste. Augustine.

—

Le Pouding de Cabinet.
La Gélée, au rhum.
Les Méringues, à la Chantilly.

—

Les Glaces de Crême, à la Portugaise.
Les Quatre Mendiants.
Les Fruits.
Le Café, etc.

L'Hôtel New York,
Mercredi, le 5 Janvier, 1859.

Just at this time three charming men visited New York and were fêted by my little circle of friends. They were Lord Frederick Cavendish, Hon. Evelyn Ashley, and G. W. des Voeux, now Governor of Hong Kong; three of the brightest spirits I had ever met, and without the slightest pretension; in fact, just what the real English gentleman always is,—the first gentleman in the world. Fearing a cold winter, and a friend who was going off on a foreign mission offering me his furnished house in Savannah, with all his servants, etc., I took it on a lease and proposed leaving for my native city in January. Finding my English friends also going South, I invited them to pass a month with me in my Southern home. All my European purchases, my china, glass, and bric-à-brac, I did not even unbale in New York, but shipped them directly to Savannah. Before leaving I took the precaution to order my marketing from old Waite of Amity Street (the then famous butcher), to be sent to me weekly, and started my new Southern household.

I naturally prided myself, on appearing in my native city, in putting my best foot foremost, and entertaining as well as I knew how, or, rather, in giving to my Southern friends, the benefit of my European education in the way of dinner giving. I found this, at first, instead of gratifying my father's friends rather piqued them; they said—"Heydey! here is a young fellow coming out here to show us how to live. Why, his father did not pretend to do this. Let us let him severely alone," which for a time they did. I took up the young fry, who let their elders very soon know that I had certainly learned something and that Mc's dinners were bound to be a feature in Savannah. Then the old patriarch of the place relented and asked me to a grand dinner.

The papers had announced the intended visit to Savannah of the son of the Duke of Devonshire, and the son of the Earl of Shaftesbury. Southern people then worshipped the English nobility. They prided themselves on retaining all the old English habits and customs, and of being descendants of the greatest nation of the world,—excepting their own. The host at the dinner announced the coming of these distinguished men, and wondered who in Savannah would have the honor of entertaining them. The British Consul then spoke up, he was a great character there, giving the finest dinners, and being an authority on wine, i.e. Madeira, "Her Majesty's Consul will have the honor." I secretly smiled, as I knew they were coming to me, and I expected them the next day. This same good old Consul had ignored me, hearing I had had the audacity to give at my table *filet de bœuf aux truffes et champignons.* I returned home feeling sure that these young noblemen would be but a few hours under my roof before Her Majesty's Consul would give me the honor of a visit. In fact, my guests had not been with me an hour when my old friend, the Consul, rushed up my front steps. Meeting me at the door he threw his arms around my neck, exclaiming, "My dear boy, I was in love with your mother thirty years ago; you are her image; carry me to your noble guests." Ever after I had the respect and esteem of this dear old man, who, for Savannah, was rich as Crœsus, and before all things esteemed and valued a good dinner and a fine glass of Madeira. My *filets de bœuf*, and the scions of noble English houses placed me in the front social rank in that little, aristocratic town, and brought forth from one of its oldest inhabitants the exclamation, "My dear boy, your aunts, the Telfairs, could give breakfasts, but you, you can give dinners."

Knowing the Englishmen's habits, I gave to each one of them, on their arrival, enormous cedar wash-tubs and hot sheets for their morning ablutions; then a good breakfast, after which we drove to the river and had my brother-in-law's ten-oared boat, called "The Rice Bird," all the oarsmen in yachting rig, myself at the tiller, and the darkeys, knowing they would all have tobacco, or money, pulled for dear life from the start to the finish, giving us their plantation songs. The leader improvised his song, the others only singing in chorus. On these occasions, the colored people would give you in song all the annoyances they were subjected to, and the current events of plantation life, bringing in much of and about their "Massa" and his family, as follows: "Massa Ward marry our little Miss Sara, bring big buckra to Savannah, gwine to be good times, my boys, pull boys, pull, over Jordan!" Reaching the plantations, of which there were three, Fairlawn, Argyle, and Shaftesbury, well equipped with admirable dogs (for my brother-in-law was a great sportsman), we would shoot snipe over the rice lands until 2 P.M., then lunch elaborately in his plantation house, and row back in the cool of the afternoon, dining at 8 o'clock, and having as my guests every pretty girl within a hundred miles and more of the city. The flowers, particularly the rose called the Cloth of Gold, and the black rose, I was most prodigal with. I had given a fee to the clerk of the market to scour the country for game and delicacies, so our dinners were excellent, and the old Southern habit of sitting over Madeira until the small hours was adopted, and was, with the bright minds I had brought together, most enjoyable.

Chapter Eight – Merrymaking in the South

In a small place, life is monotonous if you do not in some way break up this monotony. I bethought me of a friend who lived some distance from Savannah, who had a deer park, was a sportsman, and was also the soul of hospitality. His pride lay in his family and his surroundings; so I wrote to him as follows: "My dear friend, I have no baronial mansion; I am a wanderer on the face of the earth, while you possess what I most covet, an ancestral home and a great domain. Will you then invite my guests and me to pay you a visit and give us a chance at your deer?" Back came the invitation: "Come to me at once with your noble friends. I and my whole county will receive them and do them honor." The next morning, by ten, we were at the railway station. Before leaving the carriage I saw a distinguished General, a sort of Dalgetty of a man, who preferred to fight than eat, pacing up and down the railway platform. A ruffled shirt, not spotless, a fierce air, an enormous false diamond pin, as big as a crown piece, in the center of his ruffled shirt bosom, with a thin gold chain attached to it and to his waistcoat, to prevent its loss. He at once approached me and exclaimed, "By Jove! by Jove! Mc, introduce me to your noble friends." The introduction made, he accompanied us to the train, and in turn presented us to a large crowd assembled to see what Southern people were so proud of, "thoroughbreds," as he called them. I repeatedly heard him exclaim, "No jackass stock here, sir; all thoroughbreds! I could tell 'em in the dark." On rolled the train, and we soon reached our destination, and were no sooner out of the cars than we were enveloped by a myriad of sand flies. You could cut them with a knife, as it were. My friend, a six-footer, stepped up to my guests and was presented. He then addressed them as follows: "Will your lordships ride or drive?"

In the mean while, his coachman, a seedy old darkey, in a white hat at least ten years old, fly specked to such an extent that its original color was lost, in shabby, old, well-worn clothes, seized me by the coat tail, exclaiming, "Massa Ward, show me the 'big buckras.'" After pointing them out, we all pressed through the crowd to the wagon and horses, two marsh tackeys, with their manes and tails so full of burrs, and so netted together, as to form a solid mass; stirrup leathers pieced with clothes lines, and no evidence of either of the animals having ever seen or been touched by a curry-comb. "Don Quixote, by Jove!" exclaimed the heir of the Shaftesburys, and vaulted into the saddle, while the representative of the house of Devonshire and myself took our seats in the open wagon. At this point, our hospitable host called the attention of his lordship to his horses and gave him their pedigree. One was sixteen hands high, had a bob tail, and high action; the other was a little pony of fourteen hands, with an ambling gait. Not giving any sign of moving, our host held forth as follows: "Your lordship, so well bred are these horses that if they are not properly caparisoned, nothing human could stir them; they will plant their feet in the soil and neither whip nor spur would budge them. You see how well my boy keeps their harnesses." By this time I was convulsed. Cavendish, I saw, was laughing inwardly, but suppressed it. The straw in one collar was bulging out, one turret was gone, and a piece of rope lengthened one of the traces. Truly, it had seen better days. If he calls that a fitting harness for his horses, what am I to expect in the way of a house and deer park? However, my fears were allayed. The house was a charming old Southern plantation house, and the owner of it, the embodiment of hospitality. When the cloth was removed at dinner, I trembled. For my dear old father had always told me that on his circuit (annually made by the Savannah lawyers) he always avoided this house, for in it one could never find so much as a glass of whiskey. What then was my surprise, to have placed before us a superb bottle of sherry, since world-renowned, i.e. in this country; and a matchless Madeira, which he claimed he had inherited from his father, to be opened at the marriage of his sister.

The next morning, at the very break of day fixed for our deer hunt, the negro boys commenced tooting horns. As soon as I could see, I looked out of my windows and there saw four old lean, lank dogs, lifeless looking creatures, and four marsh tackeys, decorated, front and rear, with an abundance of burrs. Off we went, as sorry a looking company as one's eye had ever seen, with a crowd of half-naked children following the procession. We were out eight hours, went through swamp after swamp, our tackeys up to their fetlocks in mud, and sorry a deer did we see. One wild turkey flew over us, which my host's colored huntsman killed, the only man in the party who could shoot at all.

Returning to Savannah, we went after quail. One morning, being some fourteen miles from the city, we felt famished, having provided no lunch basket. I asked a friend, who was shooting with us and acting as our guide, if there was a white man's house within a mile or two where we could get a biscuit. He replied, "No, not one."

I pressed the matter, saying, "We must have a bite of something," and urged him to think again. He reflected, and then said, as if to himself, "Oh, no use to go there, we will get nothing." I took him up at once.

"What do you refer to," I said. "Oh," he replied, "there is a white man who lives within a mile of us, but he is the meanest creature that lives and will have nothing to give us."

"Who is he?" I exclaimed. He gave me his name. "What," said I, "Mr. Jones, who goes to Newport every summer?" "The same," said he; "do you know him?"

"Know him?" I answered, "why, man, I know no one else. He has for years asked me to visit his plantation. He lives like a prince. I saw him at a great fête at Ochre Point, Newport, several years ago. He turned up his nose at everything there, saying to me, 'Why, my dear fellow, these people don't know how to live. This fête is nothing to what I can do, at my place. Why, sir, I have so much silver I dare not keep it in my house. The vaults of the State Bank of Georgia are filled with my silver. This fête may be well enough here, but come to me at the South, come to my plantation, and I will show you what a fête is. I will show you how to live.'" My friend listened to all this with astonishment.

"Well," said he, "I have nothing to say. That is 'big' talk. Go on to your friend's place and see what you will find." On we moved, four as hungry men as you could well see. We reached the plantation, on which we found a one-story log cabin, with a front piazza, one large center room, and two shed rooms. There was a small yard, inclosed with pine palings to keep out the pigs, who were ranging about and ineffectually trying to gain an entrance. We entered the house, and, seeing an old colored man, my Southern friend opened on the old darkey with: "Where is your master?"

"In Savannah, sir."

"When does he dine?"

"At six o'clock, sir."

"What have you got for his dinner, old man?"

"Pea pie."

"Is that all that he has for his dinner?"

"Yes, sir."

"What is pea pie?" I asked.

"Cow peas and bacon," was the answer.

With this, my Southern friend stepped to the back door of the house, asked the old man to point him out a fat turkey. The old darkey did this, saying,

"There's one, sir, but, Lord help me, Massa, don't kill him."

The protest came too late. Up to the shoulder went the gun, and down fell the turkey. Now, turning to the old darkey, he said:

"Old man, pick that turkey and roast him, and tell your Massa four big buckra men are coming to dine with him to-day, at six o'clock." We got some corn-bread from the kitchen and went off shooting. A few minutes before six, we returned, and heard indeed a racket in that old cabin. The "Massa" was there, as we saw by the buggy, standing in the front yard; the horse browsing a few feet off, the harness in the buggy, and the master shouting out, "You tell me white men came here, kill my turkey, tell you to cook him, and you don't know them? Who in the devil can they be?" No sooner had he got this out, when I appeared on the scene. Up went his arms in astonishment.

"Why, Mc., is this you? Glad to see you and your friends."

Down we sat at his table, and had a dinner of small rice, pea pie, and roast turkey, washed down by a bottle of fine old Madeira, which he called "the blood of his ancestors." I looked in vain for a side-board to put silver on, or any evidence of any past fête having been given on the premises. Our host was a thoroughly local man; one of those men who, when in Paris, would say, "I'm going to town," when he proposed returning to Savannah, which, at that time, was to him the metropolis of America. This gentleman then, like others in the South, cultivated the belief that they alone lived well, and that there was no such thing as good society in New York or other Northern cities; that New Yorkers and Northern people were simply a lot of tradespeople, having no antecedents, springing up like the mushroom, who did not know how to live, and who, when they gave dinners to their friends, ordered them from a neighboring restaurant.

At a large dinner in Savannah, given to an ex-Mayor of New York, one of the best dinner-givers in that city made the foregoing statement, and the ex-Mayor actually called upon me to substantiate it, declaring it had always been his practice thus to supply his table, when he invited a dozen or more people to dinner. So far from this being the case, I then and there assured my Southern friends that no people in the world lived better than New Yorkers, so far as creature comforts were concerned. I have tested the capacity of the Southern cook alongside of the French *chef*; I had them together, cooking what we call a "Saratoga Lake Dinner" at Newport, a dinner for sixty people; serving alone Spanish mackerel, Saratoga potatoes, soft shell crabs, woodcock, chicken partridges, and lettuce salad. Both were great artists in their way, but the *chef* came off very much the victor. I doubted then, and I doubt now, if the dinners in London are better than our New York dinners, given by one of the innumerable good dinner-givers. Our material is better in New York, and our cooks are equally as good as those in England. The sauces of the French cuisine are its feature, while there is not a single sauce in African or Southern cooking. The French get the essence and flavor out of fowl, and discard the huge joints. Take for instance, soup; give a colored cook a shin of beef and a bunch of carrots and turnips, and of this he makes a soup. A Frenchman, to give you a *consommé royale*, requires a knuckle of veal, a shin of beef, two fat fowls, and every vegetable known to man. The materials are more than double the expense, but then you have a delicacy of flavor, and a sifting out of everything that is coarse and gross. The *chef* is an educated, cultivated artist. The colored cook, such as nature made him, possessing withal a wonderful natural taste, and the art of making things savory, i.e. taste good. His cookery book is tradition. French *chefs* have their inspirations, are in every way almost as much inspired as writers. To illustrate this: when Henry IV. was fighting in the Pyrénées, he told his French cook to give him a new sauce. The reply was, "Where are the materials for it, your Majesty? I have nothing here but herbs and cream." "Then make a sauce from them," was the King's answer. The *chef* did this, and produced one of the best sauces in the French cuisine, known as *sauce Bearnaise*.

Having exhausted quail and snipe shooting and made a failure at deer hunting, we went on the banks of the rice plantations at night, to shoot wild ducks, as they crossed the moon. Whilst whiling away the time, waiting for ducks, we talked over England and America. Lord Frederick Cavendish assured me that if I were then living in England, I could not there lead a pleasanter life than I was then leading. He liked everything at the South, the hospitality of the people, and their simple contentment and satisfaction with their surroundings. On these three places there were then six hundred slaves; the net income of these estates was $40,000 a year. They would have easily brought half a million. When the Civil War terminated, my brother-in-law was offered $100,000 for them; by the war he had lost all his slaves. Today the estates would scarcely bring $30,000, showing the change in values caused by the Civil War.

I was then able to show my guests a Savannah picnic, which is an institution peculiar to the place. Leaving the city in a river steamer our party consisting of one hundred people, after a little over an hour's sail we reached an island in the Atlantic Ocean, known as Dawfuskie, a beautiful spot on which stood a charming residence, with five acres of roses surrounding the house. The heads of families carried, each of them, huge baskets containing their dinner, and a full table service, wine, etc., for say, ten or a dozen people. On our arrival, all formed into groups under the trees, a cloth was laid on the ground, dishes, plates and glasses arranged on it, and the champagne at once *frapped* in small hand pails. There was then a dance in the open air, on a platform, and in the afternoon, with cushions as seats for the ladies, these improvised dinner-tables were filled. Each had its separate hostess; all was harmony and pleasure. As night approached, the people re-embarked on the steamer and returned home by moonlight.

Chapter Nine – Life at Newport

My English friends bidding me farewell, soon after, I gave up my Savannah house and made Newport my permanent home, for I spent nine months of the year there, with a winter trip to the West Indies. I must not omit to mention here that while passing the winter at Nassau, N. P., I made the acquaintance of a most polished, elegant, and courtly man, a captain in the British Navy, who entertained me as one can only be entertained on a British man-of-war, giving me Devonshire cream and every luxury, and all as well served as though it had been ashore. Meeting him repeatedly at dinner at the house of the Governor of the Bahamas, he suggested that as it was a most difficult thing to board the steamship that was to take us to New York, she never crossing the bar, he would himself, in his own gig, take us out to that vessel when we left the island.

I had forgotten this kind promise, but on the day fixed for our departure (it then blowing a gale, one of those terrible "northers" of the West Indies), I received a note from this gallant captain, telling me that his boat's crew had already crossed the bar, boarded our steamer, and learnt the precise spot where she would lie in the afternoon when she would take on her passengers. In vain did I protest against his undertaking this dangerous piece of work. Do it he would; and taking the tiller himself, we were safely rowed in his gig, twelve miles, and boarded the vessel.

I afterwards learned that while he was going from his vessel in full evening dress, with his white gloves carefully buttoned (for he was called the dandy of the English Navy), he sprang overboard and saved one of his men from drowning.

On our reaching the deck of the steamer, I was struck with the obsequiousness of the steamer's captain to the naval officer, (she was, by the way, a Cunarder). My friend, the captain, then introduced me to one of his countrymen, saying to me, simply, "You will find him a nice fellow." He turned out to be one of the most distinguished young men in England, an officer of the Household Troops, a most fascinating man, who had been to Jamaica to look after his father's estates there. I introduced him to my friends in New York, and in return for the hospitality extended to him then, heard later that he, on receiving letters of introduction from me, had paid marked attention to the bearers of the letters. I relate this as an evidence that Englishmen do reciprocate attentions received in this country.

Newport was now at its best. The most charming people of the country had formed a select little community there; the society was small, and all were included in the gaieties and festivities. Those were the days that made Newport what it was then and is now, the most enjoyable and luxurious little island in America. The farmers of the island even seemed to catch the infection, and they were as much interested in the success of our picnics and country dinners, as we were ourselves. They threw open their houses to us, and never heeded the invasion, on a bright sunshiny day, of a party of fifty people, who took possession of their dining-room, in fact of their whole house, and frolicked in it to their heart's content. To be sure, I had often to pacify a farmer when a liveried groom robbed his hen roost, but as he knew that this fashionable horde paid their way, he was easily soothed. I always then remarked that in Newport, at that time, you could have driven a four-in-hand of camels or giraffes, and the residents of the island would have smiled and found it quite the thing. The charm of the place then was the simple way of entertaining; there were no large balls; all the dancing and dining was done by daylight, and in the country. I did not hesitate to ask the very *crème de la crème* of New York society to lunch and dine at my farm, or to a fishing party on the rocks. My little farm dinners gained such a reputation that my friends would say to me: "Now, remember, leave me out of your ceremonious dinners as you choose, but always include me in those given at your farm, or I'll never forgive you." But to convey any idea of our country parties, one must in detail give the method of getting them up: Riding on the Avenue on a lovely summer's day, I would be stopped by a beautiful woman, in gorgeous array, looking so fascinating that if she were to ask you to attempt the impossible, you would at least make the effort. She would open on me as follows: "My dear friend, we are all dying for a picnic. Can't you get one up for us?"

"Why, my dear lady," I would answer, "you have dinners every day, and charming dinners too; what more do you want?"

"Oh, they're not picnics. Any one can give dinners," she would reply; "what we want is one of your picnics. Now, my dear friend, do get one up."

This was enough to fire me, and set me going. So I reply:

"I will do your bidding. Fix on the day at once, and tell me what is the best dish your cook makes."

Out comes my memorandum book, and I write: "Monday, 1 P.M., meet at Narragansett Avenue, bring *filet de bœuf piqué*," and with a bow am off in my little wagon, and dash on, to waylay the next cottager, stop every carriage known to contain friends, and ask them, one and all, to join our country party, and assign to each of them the providing of a certain dish and a bottle of champagne. Meeting young men, I charge them to take a bottle of champagne, and a pound of grapes, or order from the confectioner's a quart of ice cream to be sent to me. My pony is put on its mettle; I keep going the entire day getting recruits; I engage my music and servants, and a carpenter to put down a dancing platform, and the florist to adorn it, and that evening I go over in detail the whole affair, map it out as a general would a battle, omitting nothing, not even a salt spoon; see to it that I have men on the road to direct my party to the farm, and bid the farmer put himself and family, and the whole farm, in holiday attire.

On one occasion, as my farmer had just taken unto himself a bride, a young and pretty woman, I found that at mid-day, to receive my guests, she had dressed herself in bridal array; she was *décolleté*, and seemed quite prepared to sing the old ballad of "Coming thro' the rye"; but as her husband was a stalwart young fellow, and extremely jealous, I advised the young men in the party to confine their attentions to their own little circle and let Priscilla, the Puritan, alone.

When I first began giving picnics at my farm, I literally had no stock of my own. I felt that it would never do to have a gathering of the brightest and cleverest people in the country at my place with the pastures empty, neither a cow nor a sheep; so my Yankee wit came to my assistance. I at once hired an entire flock of Southdown sheep, and two yoke of cattle, and several cows from the neighboring farm, for half a day, to be turned into my pasture lots, to give the place an animated look. I well remember some of my knowing guests, being amateur farmers, exclaiming:

"Well, it is astonishing! Mc has but fifty acres, and here he is, keeping a splendid flock of Southdowns, two yoke of cattle, to say nothing of his cows!"

I would smile and say:

"My friend I am not a fancy farmer, like yourself; I farm for profit."

At that time, I was out of pocket from three to four thousand dollars a year by my farm, but must here add, for my justification, that finding amateur farming an expensive luxury, I looked the matter squarely in the face,

33

watched carefully the Yankee farmers around me, and satisfied myself that they knew more about the business than I did, and at once followed in their footsteps, placed my farm on shares, paying nothing out for labor, myself paying the running expenses, and dividing the profits with my farmer. Instead of losing three or four thousand dollars a year by my farm, it then paid me, and continues to pay me seven to eight hundred dollars a year clear of all expenses. We sell off of fifty acres of land, having seventeen additional acres of pasturage, over three thousand dollars of produce each year. I sell fifty Southdown lambs during the months of April and May, at the rate of eight to ten dollars each, to obtain which orders are sent to me in advance, and my winter turkeys have become as famous as my Southdown lambs. The farm is now a profit instead of a loss. I bought this place in 1853; if I had bought the same amount of land south of Newport, instead of north of the town, it would have been worth a fortune to-day.

To return to our picnic. The anxiety as to what the weather would be, was always my first annoyance, for of course these country parties hinge on the weather. After making all your preparations, everything ready for the start, then to look out of your window in the morning, as I have often done, and see the rain coming down in torrents, is far from making you feel cheerful. But, as a rule, I have been most fortunate in my weather. We would meet at Narragansett Avenue at 1 P.M., and all drive out together. On reaching the picnic grounds, I had an army of skirmishers, in the way of servants, thrown out, to take from each carriage its contribution to the country dinner. The band would strike up, and off the whole party would fly in the waltz, while I was directing the icing of the champagne, and arranging the tables; all done with marvelous celerity. Then came my hour of triumph, when, without giving the slightest signal (fearing some one might forestall me, and take off the prize), I would dash in among the dancers, secure our society queen, and lead with her the way to the banquet. Now began the fun in good earnest. The clever men of the party would assert their claims to the best dishes, proud of the efforts of their cook, loud in their praise of their own game pie, which most probably was brought out by some third party, too modest to assert and push his claim. Beauty was there to look upon, and wit to enliven the feast. The wittiest of men was then in his element, and I only wish I dared quote here his brilliant sallies. The beauty of the land was also there, and all feeling that they were on a frolic, they threw hauteur, ceremonial, and grand company manners aside, and, in place, assumed a spirit of simple enjoyment. Toasts were given and drunk, then a stroll in pairs, for a little interchange of sentiment, and then the whole party made for the dancing platform, and a cotillon of one hour and a half was danced, till sunset. As at a "Meet," the arrivals and departures were a feature of the day. Four-in-hands, tandems, and the swellest of Newport turn-outs rolled by you. At these entertainments you formed lifetime intimacies with the most cultivated and charming men and women of this country.

These little parties were then, and are now, the stepping-stones to our best New York society. People who have been for years in mourning and thus lost sight of, or who having passed their lives abroad and were forgotten, were again seen, admired, and liked, and at once brought into society's fold. Now, do not for a moment imagine that all were indiscriminately asked to these little fêtes. On the contrary, if you were not of the inner circle, and were a new-comer, it took the combined efforts of all your friends' backing and pushing to procure an invitation for you. For years, whole families sat on the stool of probation, awaiting trial and acceptance, and many were then rejected, but once received, you were put on an intimate footing with all. To acquire such intimacy in a great city like New York would have taken you a lifetime. A fashionable woman of title from England remarked to me that we were one hundred years behind London, for our best society was so small, every one in it had an individuality. This, to her, was charming, "for," said she, "one could have no such individuality in London." It was accorded only to the highest titled people in all England, while here any one in society would have every movement chronicled. Your "*personnel*," she added, "is daily discussed, your equipage is the subject of talk, as well as your house and household." Another Londoner said to me, "This Newport is no place for a man without fortune." There is no spot in the world where people are more *en evidence*. It is worth while to do a thing well there, for you have people who appreciate your work, and it tells and pays. It is the place of all others to take social root in.

Chapter Ten - Society's Leaders

Society must have its leader or leaders. It has always had them, and will continue to have them. Their sway is more or less absolute. When I came to New York as a boy, forty years ago, there were two ladies who were skillful leaders and whose ability and social power the fashionable world acknowledged. They gave the handsomest balls and dinners given in this city, and had at them all the brilliant people of that period. Their suppers, given by old Peter Van Dyke, were famous. Living in two adjoining houses which communicated, they had superb rooms for entertaining. These were the days when Isaac Brown, sexton of Grace Church, was, in his line, a great character. His memory was something remarkable. He knew all and everything about everybody, knew always every one's residence, was good-nature itself, and cracked his jokes and had a word for every one who passed into the ballroom. You would hear him *sotto voce* remarking upon men as they passed: "Old family, good old stock," or "He's a new man; he had better mind his p's and q's, or I will trip him up. Ah, here's a fellow who intends to dance his way into society. Here comes a handsome boy, the women are crazy about him," etc.

A year or two later, during my absence in Europe and at the South, a lady living in Washington Place found herself filling a very conspicuous place in the matter of social entertainment by the departure of her husband's relatives, who had been society's leaders, for a prolonged stay in Europe. A woman of charming manners, possessing eminently the talent of social leadership, she took up and easily carried on society as represented by the "smart" set. For from six to seven years she gave brilliant entertainments; her dinners were exquisite; her wines perfect; her husband's Madeiras are still famous. At that time, her small dances were most carefully chosen; they were the acme of exclusiveness. On this she prided herself. She also arranged and controlled for two years (the winters of 1870 and 1871) small subscription balls at Delmonico's, Fourteenth Street, in his "blue rooms." They were confined to the young men and maidens, with the exception, perhaps, of a dozen of the young married couples; a few elderly married ladies were invited as matrons. These dances were known and became famous as the "Blue Room parties." There were three hundred subscribers to them. Having a large fortune, she was able to gratify her taste in entertaining. Her manners were charming, and she was a most pleasing conversationalist. Her brother-in-law was one of the founders of the Patriarchs, and at a later period her two sons-in-law also joined them, though the younger of the two, the husband of her accomplished and beautiful daughter, has lived abroad for many years, but is still numbered among the brilliant members of our society. It was during the winter of 1871 that a ball was given in these same rooms to Prince Arthur, when on his visit here. On this occasion, the Prince danced with the daughter of my old friend, the Major, who, in air and distinction, was unrivaled in this country.

About this time two beautiful, brilliant women came to the front. They were both descended from old Colonial families. They had beauty and wealth, and were eminently fitted to lead society. A new era then came in; old fashions passed away, new ones replaced them. The French *chef* then literally, for the first time, made his appearance, and artistic dinners replaced the old-fashioned, solid repasts of the earlier period. We imported European habits and customs rapidly. Women were not satisfied with their old *modistes*, but must needs send to Paris for everything. The husband of one of these ladies had a great taste for society, and also a great knowledge of all relating to it. His delight was to see his beautiful young wife worshipped by everybody, which she was, and she soon became, in every sense, the prominent leader. All admired her, and we, the young men of that period, loved her as much as we dared. All did homage to her, and certainly she was deserving of it, for she had every charm, and never seemed to over-appreciate herself, or recognize that as Nature had lavished so much on her, and man had laid wealth at her feet, she was, in every sense, society's queen. She was a woman *sans aucune prétention*. When you entered her house, her reassuring smile, her exquisitely gracious and unpretending manner of receiving, placed you at your ease and made you feel welcome. She had the power that all women should strive to obtain, the power of attaching men to her, and keeping them attached; calling forth a loyalty of devotion such as one imagines one yields to a sovereign, whose subjects are only too happy to be subjects. In the way of entertaining, the husband stood alone. He had a handsome house and a beautiful picture gallery (which served as his ball-room), the best *chef* in the city, and entertained royally.

I well remember being asked by a member of my family, "Why are you so eager to go to this leader's house?" My reply always was, "Because I enjoy such refined and cultivated entertainments. It improves and elevates one." From him, I literally took my first lesson in the art of giving good dinners. I heard his criticisms, and well remember asking old Monnot, the keeper of the New York Hotel:

"Who do you think has the best cook in this city?"

"Why, of course, the husband of your leader of fashion, for the simple reason that he makes his cook give him a good dinner every day."

Just at this time all New York aroused, and put on their holiday attire at the coming of the Prince of Wales. A grand ball at the Academy of Music was given him. Our best people, the smart set, the slow set, all sets, took a hand in it, and the endeavor was to make it so brilliant and beautiful that it would always be remembered by those present as one of the events of their lives.

My invitation to the ball read as follows:

THE GENERAL COMMITTEE OF ARRANGEMENTS
Invite Mr. Ward McAllister to a Ball to be given by the Citizens of New York to the
PRINCE OF WALES,
At the Academy of Music, on Friday Evening, the twelfth of October, 1860, at nine o'clock.

Peter Cooper, *M. B. Field,*
Chairman.   *Secretary.*

The ball was to be opened by a *Quadrille d'Honneur*. Governor and Mrs. Morgan, Mr. Bancroft the historian, and Mrs. Bancroft, Colonel and Mrs. Abraham Van Buren, with others, were to dance in it. Mrs. Morgan had forgotten all she had learned of dancing in early childhood, so she at once took dancing lessons. Fernando Wood was then Mayor of New York. The great event of the evening was to be the opening quadrille, and the rush to be near it was so great that the floor gave way and in tumbled the whole centre of the stage. I stood up in the first tier, getting a good view of the catastrophe. The Duke of Newcastle, with the Prince, who, as it happened, was advancing to the centre of the stage, followed by all who were to dance in the quadrille, at once retired with the Prince to the reception room, while Mr. Renwick, the architect, and a gang of carpenters got to work to floor over the chasm. I well remember the enormous form of old Isaac Brown, sexton of Grace Church, rushing around and encouraging the workmen. A report had been spread that the Duke would not allow the Prince to again appear on the stage.

In the mean while, the whole royal party were conversing in groups in the reception room. The Prince had been led into a corner of the room by the Mayor's daughter, when the Duke, feeling the young lady had had fully her share of his Royal Highness, was about to interrupt them, when our distinguished magistrate implored him not to do so. "Oh, Duke," he exclaimed, "let the young people alone, they are enjoying themselves." The stage made safe, the quadrille was danced, to the amusement of the assembled people. The old-fashioned curtseys, the pigeon-wings, and genuflexions only known to our ancestors were gone through with dignity and repose. Mrs. Van Buren, who had presided over the White House during Martin Van Buren's presidency, has repeatedly since discussed this quadrille with me, declaring she was again and again on the point of laughing at the grotesque figures cut by the dancers.

"But, my dear sir," she said, "I did not permit my dignity and repose to be at all ruffled; I think I went through the trying ordeal well; but why, why will not our people learn to dance!" A waltz immediately followed the quadrille; the Prince, a remarkably handsome young man, with blue eyes and light hair, a most agreeable countenance, and a gracious manner, danced with Miss Fish, Miss Mason, Miss Fannie Butler, and others, and danced well. I followed him with a fair partner, doing all I could to enlarge the dancing circle. He danced incessantly until supper, the arrangements for which were admirable.

One entered the supper room by one stage door and left it by another; a horseshoe table ran around the entire room,—behind it stood an army of servants, elbow to elbow, all in livery. At one end of the room was a raised dais, where the royal party supped. At each stage door a prominent citizen stood guard; the moment the supper room was full, no one else was admitted. As fifty would go out, fifty would come in. I remember on my attempting to get in through one of these doors, stealthily, the vigilant eye of John Jacob Astor met mine. He bid me wait my turn. Nothing could have been more successful, or better done. The house was packed to repletion. Now, all was the Prince. The city rang with his name; all desired to catch a glimpse of him. His own people could not have offered him greater homage.

A friend of mine at Barrytown telegraphed me to come to him and pass Sunday, and on Monday go with him to West Point to a breakfast to be given by Colonel Delafield, the Commandant of the Point, to the Prince of Wales. It was in the fall of the year, when the Hudson was at its best, clothed in its autumnal tints. I was enraptured on looking out of my window on Sunday morning at the scene that lay before me, with the river, like a tiny thread away below, gracefully flowing through a wilderness of foliage, the flock of Southdown sheep on my friend's lawn, the picturesque little stone chapel adjoining his place, all in full view, and the great masses of autumn leaves raked in huge piles. Going to church in the morning, I proposed to myself a ten-mile walk in the afternoon to get an appetite for what I felt sure would be my friend's best effort in the way of a dinner, as he well knew I loved the "flesh pots of Egypt." Fully equipped for my walk, the butler entered my room and announced luncheon. I declined the meal. Again he appeared, stating that the family insisted on my lunching with them, as on Sunday it was always a most substantial repast.

My host now appeared to enforce the request. I protested. "My dear fellow, I can dine but once in twenty-four hours; dinner to me is an event; luncheon is fatal to dinner—takes off the edge of your appetite, and then you are unfit to do it justice."

"Have it as you will," he replied, and off I went. Returning, I donned my dress suit, and feeling as hungry as a hound, went to the drawing-room to await dinner. Seven came, half after seven, and still no announcement of that meal. I felt an inward sinking. At eight the butler announced "Tea is served."

"Good heavens!" I muttered to myself; "I have lost dinner," and woefully went in to tea. I can drink tea at my breakfast, but that suffices; I can never touch it a second time in twenty-four hours. I think my host took in the situation, and to intensify my suffering, walked over to me, tapping me on the back, exclaiming:

"My dear boy, in this house we never dine on Sunday."

"Why in the plague, then," I thought, "did you ask me up here on a fast day? However," I said to myself, "I will make it up on bread and butter." In we went to tea, and a tea indeed it was; what the French would call a "*Souper dinatoire*," the English, a "high tea," a combination of a heavy lunch, a breakfast, and tea. No hot dishes; but every cold delicacy you could dream of; a sort of "whipping the devil around the stump." No dinner, a gorgeous feast at tea.

Down the river the next morning we went to West Point, every moment enjoyable, and reached the Commandant's house. As General Scott was presenting Colonel Delafield's guests to the Prince I approached the General, asking him to present me to his Royal Highness. A giant as he was in height, he bent down his head to me, and asked sharply, "What name, sir?" I gave him my name, but at the sound of "Mc," not thinking it distinguished enough, he quietly said, "Pass on, sir," and I subsequently was presented by the Duke of Newcastle.

Chapter Eleven – Delights of Country Life

All my life I had been taught to have a sort of reverence for the name of Livingston, and to feel that Livingston Manor was a species of palatial residence, that one must see certainly once in one's lifetime. The opportunity offered itself, and I seized upon it. The owner of the upper Manor jokingly suggested our forming a party to go there, and take possession of his house in October, and see the lovely autumn foliage. By acclamation, it was resolved that the project be carried out, and I went to work, spurring up my old friend, the owner of the Manor, to prepare for us. As an important feature and member of this party, I must here give a slight sketch of one of the handsomest, most fascinating, most polished and courteous gentlemen of that or any other period. We will here call him the Major; amiability itself, a man both sexes could fall in love with. I loved him dearly, and when I lost him I felt much of the charm of life had departed with him. At all these country parties, he was always first and foremost. My rapidity of thought and action always annoyed him. "My dear fellow," he would say, "for heaven's sake, go slow; you tear through the streets as if at some one's bidding. A gentleman should stroll leisurely, casting his eyes in the shop windows, as if in search of amusement, while you go at a killing pace, as if on business bent. The man of fashion should have no business." Again, he had a holy horror of familiar garments. "My dear boy," he would smile and say, "when will you discard that old coat? I am so familiar with it, I am fatigued at the sight of it."

On one subject we were always in accord—our admiration for women. My eye was quicker than his, and I often took advantage of it. I would say, "Major, did you see that beauty? By Jove, a most delicious creature!"

"Who? Where?" he would exclaim.

"Why, man," I replied, "she has passed you; you have lost her."

"Lost her! How could you let that happen? Why, why did you not sooner call my attention to her?"

Apropos of the Major, I must tell a good story at his expense:

As my farm parties were always gotten up at a day's notice, I was often in straits to provide the dishes, for all that was wanting to complete the feast I furnished myself. A boned turkey, on one occasion, was absolutely necessary. The day was a holiday. I must at once place it in the cook's hands. The shops were all shut, so I suggested to the Major that he drive out with me to my farm and procure one. When we reached the place, farmer and family, we found, had gone off visiting; there was no one there. I took in the situation at a glance.

"Major," I said, "there, in that field, is a gobbler; that turkey you and I have got to catch, if it takes us all night to get him. Positively I shall not leave the place without him." He looked aghast. There he was, in Poole's clothes, the best dressed man in America! This he always was. On this point, a friend once got this off on him. As he was entering his club, with another well-dressed man of leisure, this gentleman exclaimed, "Behold them! like the lilies of the field, they toil not, neither do they spin, yet Solomon in all his glory was not arrayed like one of these." Clothes, or no clothes, in pursuit of the turkey we went. Over fences, under fences, in barnyards and through fields, at a full run, the perspiration pouring down the cheeks of the dear old Major, and I screaming encouragement to him. "Try it again, Major! head him off! now you have him!"

Finally, after an hour's chase, we got the bird, when, throwing off his coat, straightening himself up and throwing his arms akimbo, he exclaimed, "Well, Mc, the profession of a gentleman has fallen very low when it takes him to chasing turkeys."

"My dear fellow," I replied, "the great Chancellor Livingston once said, 'a gentleman can do anything; he can clean his own boots, but he should do it well.'"

To return to our excursion.

The party to go up the North River to the Manor Livingston, and ride back to New York, was at once formed. My first discussion with the Major was as to the propriety of taking a valet, he insisting it was indispensable, that every college boy in England, on three hundred pounds a year, had his valet. I contended that they were nuisances, and it was not the habit to indulge in them here. Besides this, our host would have his hands full in caring for us, and would feel we were imposing on him if each of us took a man servant. This settled it. The Major and I were to travel together and meet the party at Staatsburg. Let me here say that people of the world put up with the annoyance of travel better than any other class of people.

The glorious morning that we left the cars at Poughkeepsie, and mounted our horses, I shall never forget. That lovely ride, from Poughkeepsie to Staatsburg, under that superb row of old trees, put me in mind of the Long Walk at Windsor; it is equally as handsome. We speculated on the way as to what we were to expect. "If he has no *chef*, I leave in twenty-four hours," exclaimed my friend. I assured him we might feel secure of finding artistic cooking and of having a very jolly good time. Instead of a palace, I found a fine, old-fashioned country-house, very draughty, but beautifully placed amid magnificent forest trees. My first exploit was to set fire to the carpet in my room by building a huge fire in my grate, to try and keep warm. As the Major put it, "My dear boy, burn yourself up if you will, but kindly remember you endanger all our lives."

At eleven every morning we were all in the saddle, and went off for a ride of some twenty miles, lunching at some fine house or other. It was English life to perfection, and most enjoyable. Hyde Park, with two superbly kept places, and its little village church on a Sunday, carried you back to England, and it seemed then to me that you there found the perfection of country life.

It was whilst dining in one of these old baronial mansions, that I conceived the idea of transporting the whole party to my late father-in-law's place at Madison, New Jersey, and giving them myself, in his old residence, another country entertainment. After inviting them, I began to realize what I had undertaken. The house itself was all one could wish, built of brick, and nearly as large as the White House in Washington. But it had been shut up and unoccupied for years; however, I was in for it and I resolved, in spite of all difficulties, to carry it through successfully. After a week at the Manor, our whole party of some dozen ladies and gentlemen mounted our horses, and rode down to New York, sending the servants ahead by rail, to engage apartments,

41

have our rooms ready, and dinner prepared for us at the village inns where we were to sleep. It was amusing to see the gentlemen in dress coats and white cravats, and the ladies in their handsome toilets, sitting down in a village inn to ham and eggs and boiled chicken and cabbage; but, as we had always sent on the wine, and had the best of servants to look after everything, we enjoyed these inn dinners very much. Not a murmur from any of the ladies of any discomfort; they found everything charming and amusing. So day by day we rode, chatting away and enjoying each other's society, and at night, after a cosy little meal, we were all only too glad to seek the arms of Morpheus.

When I returned to my family at Newport and informed them of what I had done, that I had invited a dozen of the most *difficile*, fastidious people of Newport to pass ten days with us in New Jersey, at my brother-in-law's then unoccupied and shut-up residence, there was but one exclamation, "You are crazy! How could you think of such a thing! How are you to care for all these people in that old deserted house?" All they said did not discourage me. I determined to show my friends that, though the Gibbons mansion was not a Manor house, it was deserving of the name, and was, at that date, one of the handsomest, largest, most substantial, and well-built residences at the North. When the Civil War broke out, my brother-in-law requested me to make it my home.

I give in detail all I did to successfully entertain my friends for ten days in this old family house, as it may instruct others how to act in a similar case. In London, during the season, one hires a house for a few days to give a ball in, and there are many very superb large houses used there in this way every year. Telegraphing at once to the agent who had charge of this house to put an army of scrubbing-women in it, and have it cleaned from cellar to garret, I next went into the wholesale business of kerosene and lamps. In the country particularly there is nothing like an illumination *à giorno* at night. I hunted up an experienced *chef*, got my servants, and then made *menus* for ten dinners, lunches, and breakfasts, as my guests were asked for a certain length of time; engaged a country band of music for the evenings, telegraphed to Baltimore for my canvasbacks, arranged for my fish, vegetables, and flowers to be sent up by train daily from New York, purchased myself every article of food that I would require to make up these *menus*, gave orders for my ices, bonbons, and cakes, everything that must be fresh to be good, to come to me by express; sent up my wines, but no Madeira, as I knew there was enough of that wine in the wine cellars of that old house to float a frigate; looked after my stabling, and found we could stable twenty horses in a fine brick stable, and house all the drags and vehicles. The conservatories were full of orange and lemon trees. The house itself, architecturally, was a duplicate of the White House in Washington, and almost as large. It had a superb marble hall, 20 × 45, leading to a dining-room, 36 × 25. The house was built in 1836, of brick, in a forest of trees, with the three farms surrounding it really forming part of the grounds, containing a thousand acres of land. The house and grounds cost in 1836 over $150,000. All I had to do, then, was to reanimate the interior and take from hidden recesses the fine old family china, and the vast quantity of silver accumulated in the family for three generations. My wife's grandfather had been a distinguished lawyer; being wealthy, he had some of his lawyer's fees which were paid in Spanish dollars, melted into plate. I only wish it had been my good fortune to have secured some of those old grand silver salvers.

Before a guest arrived, everything on and about the place had life and animation. To all my guests the house was a surprise, for it had never before been shown to fashionable people. As on the North River, we passed the days in the saddle, and driving four-in-hands, lunched with many distinguished people, at their distant country places, and lived for those ten days as thoroughly an English life as one would have lived at a country house in England. I had invited young men to come down from New York every evening to join us at dinner, and even the fastidious and exacting Major, I think, was satisfied with everything. The success of this party evidenced that a country house can be made as perfect and enjoyable here as in any other country, provided you will take the trouble and bear the expense. Now, Newport life is wholly and entirely a contrast to all this, for the charm of that place is its society. You do not bring it there, but find it there, and it takes care of itself, and comes to you when you wish it; thus you are relieved of the care of providing daily for a large company, to do which is well enough in England, where you inherit your servants with your fortune, while here, to have things properly done, be you who you may, you must give them your time and attention. This country party I gave in November, 1862.

Chapter Twelve – Fashionable People

Meeting John Van Buren as I left the cars in Jersey City to cross the ferry to New York, he insisted on my dining with him that day at the Union Club, to meet Lord Hartington, and his brother, Lord Edward Cavendish, to whom he was giving a large dinner. I declined, as I had no dress-suit in the city, but he would not take no for an answer.

"My dear man," he said, "it will be an event in your life to meet these distinguished men. Jump in the first train, return to your country home, and get your dress-coat. By all means you must not miss my dinner." As I knew Lord Frederick Cavendish so well, I really wanted to meet his brothers, and as no one could send me my spike-tail coat as they call it at the South, I took a way train and consumed the entire day getting the necessary outfit, and returning with it to the city. To compensate me for my day's work, Van Buren put me next to Lord Hartington. Chatting with him, I asked him what he had seen in our habits, manners, and speech that struck him as odd. At first he avoided making any criticism, but finally he laughingly replied, "The way you all have of saying 'Yes, sir,' or 'No, sir.' We never do this in England; it is used thus only by servants." James Brady, a great chum of our host's, being at the dinner, kept up an incessant fire at Van Buren, who retaliated with, "My dear Lord Hartington, pay no attention to what my friend Brady says; all I can say of him is that he is a man who passes one half his time in defending criminals and the other half in assailing patriots, such as myself." I was well repaid for all the trouble I had taken to attend this dinner.

At this time there were not more than one or two men in New York who spent, in living and entertaining, over sixty thousand dollars a year. There were not half a dozen *chefs* in private families in this city. Compare those days to these, and see how easily one or two men of fortune could then control, lead, and carry on society, receive or shut out people at their pleasure. If distinguished strangers failed to bring letters to them, they were shut out from everything. Again, if, though charming people, others were not in accord with those powers, they could be passed over and left out of society. All this many of us saw, and saw how it worked, and we resolved to band together the respectable element of the city, and by this union make such strength that no individual could withstand us. The motto, we felt, must be *nous nous soutenons*. This motto we then assumed, and we hold it to this day, and have found that the good and wise men of this community could always control society. This they have done and are still doing. Our first step then in carrying out these views was to arrange for a series of "cotillion dinners."

I must here explain, that behind what I call the "smart set" in society, there always stood the old, solid, substantial, and respected people. Families who held great social power as far back as the birth of this country, who were looked up to by society, and who always could, when they so wished, come forward and exercise their power, when, for one reason or another, they would take no active part, joining in it quietly, but not conspicuously. Ordinarily, they preferred, like the gods, to sit upon Olympus. I remember a lady, the head of one of these families, stating to me that she had lived longer in New York society than any other person. This point, however, was not yielded or allowed to go undisputed, for the daughter of a rival house contended that *her* family had been longer in New York society than any other family, and though she had heard the assertion, as I gave it, she would not admit its correctness. What I intend to convey is that the heads of these families, feeling secure in their position, knowing that they had great power when they chose to exercise it, took no leading part in society's daily routine. They gave handsome dinners, and perhaps, once a year, a fine ball. I know of one or two families who have scrupulously all their lives avoided display, anything that could make fashionable people of them, holding their own, esteemed and respected, and when they threw open their doors to society, all made a rush to enter. To this day, if one of these old families, even one of its remotest branches, gives a day reception, you will find the street in which they live blockaded with equipages.

For years we have literally had but one *salon* in this city—a gathering in the evening of all the brilliant and cultivated people, both young and old, embracing the distinguished strangers. A most polished and cultivated Bostonian, a brilliant woman, was the first, in my day, to receive in this way weekly. During her life she held this *salon*, both here, and all through the summer in Newport. "The robe of Elijah fell upon Elisha" in an extremely talented woman of the world, who has most successfully held, and now holds, this *salon*, on the first day of every week during the winter, and at Newport in summer.

The mistake made by the world at large is that fashionable people are selfish, frivolous, and indifferent to the welfare of their fellow-creatures; all of which is a popular error, arising simply from a want of knowledge of the true state of things. The elegancies of fashionable life nourish and benefit art and artists; they cause the expenditure of money and its distribution; and they really prevent our people and country from settling down into a humdrum rut and becoming merely a money-making and money-saving people, with nothing to brighten up and enliven life; they foster all the fine arts; but for fashion what would become of them? They bring to the front merit of every kind; seek it in the remotest corners, where it modestly shrinks from observation, and force it into notice; adorn their houses with works of art, and themselves with all the taste and novelty they can find in any quarter of the globe, calling forth talent and ingenuity. Fashionable people cultivate and refine themselves, for fashion demands this of them. Progress is fashion's watchword; it never stands still; it always advances, it values and appreciates beauty in woman and talent and genius in man. It is certainly always most charitable; it surrounds itself with the elegancies of life; it soars, it never crawls. I know the general belief is that all fashionable people are hollow and heartless. My experience is quite the contrary. I have found as warm, sympathetic, loving hearts in the garb of fashion as out of it. A thorough acquaintance with the world enables them to distinguish the wheat from the chaff, so that all the good work they do is done with knowledge and effect. The world could not dispense with it. Fashion selects its own votaries. You will see certain members of a family born to it, as it were, others of the same family with none of its attributes. You can give no explanation of this; "One is taken, the other left." Such and such a man or woman are cited as having been always fashionable. The talent of and for society develops itself just as does the talent for art.

Chapter Thirteen - Cotillions in Doors and Out

But to return to our Cotillion Dinners. A friend thought they were impracticable on account of the expense, but I had remembered talking to the proprietor of the famous Restaurant Phillipe in Paris, as to the cost of a dinner, he assuring me that its cost depended entirely on what he called *les primeurs*, i.e. things out of season, and said that he could give me, for a napo-leon a head, an excellent dinner, if I would leave out *les primeurs*. Including them, the same dinner would cost three napoleons. "I can give you, for in-stance," he said, "a *filet de bœuf aux ceps* at half the cost of a *filet aux truffes*, and so on, through the dinner, can reduce the expense." Submitting all this to my friend Delmonico, I suggested a similar inexpensive dinner, and figured the whole expense down until I reduced the cost of a cotillion dinner for sev-enty-five or a hundred people to ten dollars each person, music and every expense included. Calling on my friends, they seconded me, and we then had a winter of successful cotillion dinners. It was no easy task, however. How I was beset by the men to give them the women of their choice to take in to dinner! and in turn by the ladies not to inflict on them an uncongenial part-ner. The largest of these dinners, consisting of over a hundred people, we gave at Delmonico's, corner of Fifth Avenue and Fourteenth Street, in the large ball-room. The table was in the shape of a horseshoe. I stood at the door of the *salon*, naming to each man the lady he was to take in to dinner, and well remember one of them positively refusing to accept and take in a lady assigned to him; and she, just entering, heard the dispute, and, in conse-quence, would never again attend one of these dinners. Sitting at the head of the table, with the two young and beautiful women who were then the *grandes dames* of that time, one on either side of me, we had opposite to us, on the other side of the narrow, horseshoe table, a young blonde bride, who had just entered society. I well remember the criticisms these grand la-dies made of and about her. The one, turning to me, said, "And this is your lovely blonde, the handsomest blonde in America!" The other, the best judge of her sex that I have ever seen, then cast her horoscope, saying, "I consider her as beautiful a blonde as I have ever seen. That woman, be assured, will have a brilliant career. Such women are rare." These words were prophetic, for that beautiful bride, crossing the ocean in her husband's yacht, wholly and solely by her beauty gained for her husband and herself a brilliant posi-tion in London society. Turning to me, the lady who had made this remark asked me how she herself looked. I replied, "Like Venus rising from the sea." My serenity was here disturbed by finding that one of the ladies, disliking her next neighbor, as soon as she discovered by the card who it was, had quietly made an exchange of cards, depriving a young gallant of the seat he most coveted, and for which he had long and earnestly prayed. Of course, I was called to explain, and quiet the disturbed waters. The gentleman was furious, and threatened dire destruction to the culprit. I took in the situation, and protected the fair lady by sacrificing the waiter. After the ladies left the table, at these dinners, the gentlemen were given time to smoke a cigar and take their coffee. On this occasion, the Earl of Roseberry was a guest. Whilst smoking and commenting on the dinner, he said to me, "You Americans have made a mistake; your emblematic bird should have been a canvasback, not an eagle."

It was either to this distinguished man or the Earl of Cork, at one of these after-dinner conversations, that I held forth on the treatment of venison, asserting that here, we always serve the *saddle* of venison, whilst in England they give the *haunch*. And when they send it off to a friend, they box it up in a long narrow box, much resembling a coffin. The reason for this was given me,—that their dinners were larger than ours, and there was not enough on a saddle for an English dinner. Again, I called attention to the fact that here we eat the tenderloin steak, there they eat the rump steak, which we give to our servants. The reason for this, I was told, was that they killed their cattle younger than we killed ours, and did not work those intended for beef. On Madeira, I stated, "we had them," for, I said, "You have none to liken unto ours"; though later on, at another dinner, when I made this assertion, the Duke of Beaufort took me up on this point, and insisted upon it that in many of the old country houses in England they had excellent Madeira.

The following anonymous lines on this dinner were sent to me the day afterwards:

> There ne'er was seen so fair a sight
> As at Delmonico's last night;
> When feathers, flowers, gems, and lace
> Adorned each lovely form and face;
> A garden of all thorns bereft,
> The outside world behind them left.
> They sat in order, as if "Burke"
> Had sent a message by his clerk.
> And by whose magic wand is this
> All conjured up? the height of bliss.
> 'Tis he who now before you looms,—
> The Autocrat of Drawing Rooms.

One of the events of this winter was a grand domino ball, the largest ever given here. Our Civil War was then raging; a distinguished nobleman appeared at that ball with his friend, a member of Parliament. Before he could enter the ball-room, a domino stepped up to him and had an encounter of words with him. "Are you as brave as you look?" she asked; "will you do a woman's bidding? I challenge you to grant me my request!" "What is it?" he asked. "Allow me to pin on this badge?" "Certainly," was the gallant reply. As he passed through the rooms, it was seen that he was wearing a Secession badge. It was thought to be an intended affront to Northern people, and was immediately resented. His friend, the member of Parliament, hearing of it, at once went up to him and removed the badge. Many felt that this distinguished man was simply the victim of a cruel, mischievous, and silly woman.

The following summer, as I had been so hospitably entertained in Nassau, at Government House, I invited my old friend, the Governor of the Bahamas, to pay me a visit at Newport. On a beautiful summer afternoon, I drove up to the Brevoort House, and there I found him literally surrounded by all his worldly goods, his entire household, with all their effects. It took two immense stages and a huge baggage wagon to convey them to the Fall River boat. Imagine this party coming from an island where it was a daily struggle to procure food, viewing the sumptuous supper-tables of these magnificent steamers (which certainly made a great impression on them, for it caused them to be loud in their expressions of astonishment and admiration). Reaching Newport at 2 A.M., on attempting to go ashore, I found His Excellency had lost all his tickets. Our sharp Yankee captain took no stock in people who did such things; so out came the Englishman's pocket-book to pay again for the entire party, the dear old gentleman declaring it was his fault, and he ought to be made to pay for such carelessness. It did not take me long to convince our captain that we were not sharpers; that we had paid our passages, and we must needs be allowed to go ashore.

I was determined to evidence to my guests that they had reached the land of plenty, and before they had been with me a week, the Governor declared, with a sigh, "That he detested the sight of food." I put him through a course of vapor baths, and galloped him daily. On one occasion, we visited the beach together, when the surf was full of people. We saw an enormously tall, Rubens-like woman, clad in a clinging garment of calico, exhilarated by the bath, jumping up and down, and in her ecstasy throwing her arms up over her head. "Who is the creature?" he exclaimed. "Is this allowed here! Why, man, you should not tolerate it a moment!" I gave one look at the female, and then, convulsed with laughter, seized his arm, exclaiming, "It is your wife's English maid!" If I had given him an electric shock, he could not have sprung out of the wagon quicker. Rushing to the water's edge, he shouted, "Down with you! down with you, this instant, you crazy jade! how dare you disgrace me in this way!" The poor girl, one could see, felt innocent of all wrong, but quitted the water at lightning speed when she saw the crowd the Governor had drawn around him.

The first Cotillion Dinner ever given at Newport, I gave at my Bayside Farm. I chose a night when the moon would be at the full, and invited guests enough to make up a cotillion. We dined in the open air at 6 P.M., in the garden adjoining the farm-house, having the gable end of the house to protect us from the southerly sea breeze. In this way we avoided flies, the pest of Newport. In the house itself we could not have kept them from the table, while in the open air even a gentle breeze, hardly perceptible, rids you of them entirely. The farm-house kitchen was then near at hand for use. You sat on closely cut turf, and with the little garden filled with beautiful standing plants, the eastern side of the farm-house covered with vines, laden with pumpkins, melons, and cucumbers, all giving a mixture of bright color against a green background, with the whole farm lying before you, and beyond it the bay and the distant ocean, dotted over with sailing craft, the sun, sinking behind the Narragansett hills, bathing the Newport shore in golden light, giving you, as John Van Buren then said to me, "As much of the sea as you ever get from the deck of a yacht." Add to this, the exquisite toilets which our women wear on such occasions, a table laden with every delicacy, and all in the merriest of moods, and you have a picture of enjoyment that no shut-in ball-room could present. No "pent-up Utica" then confined our powers. Men and women enjoyed a freedom that their rural surroundings permitted, and, like the lambs gambolling in the fields next them, they frisked about, and thus did away with much of the stiff conventionality pertaining to a city entertainment.

On this little farm I had a cellar for claret and a farm-house attic for Madeira, where the cold Rhode Island winters have done much to preserve for me wines of seventy and eighty years of age. On this occasion, I remember giving them Amory of 1811 (one of the greatest of Boston Madeiras), and I saw the men hold it up to the light to see its beautiful amber color, inhale its bouquet, and quaff it down "with tender eyes bent on them."

A marked feature of all my farm dinners was *Dindonneaux à la Toulouse*, and *à la Bordelaise* (chicken turkeys). In past days, turkeys were thought to be only fine on and after Thanksgiving Day in November, but I learnt from the French that the turkey *poult* with *quenelle de volaille*, with either a white or dark sauce, was the way to enjoy the Rhode Island turkey. I think they were first served in this way on my farm in Newport. Now they are thus cooked and accepted by all as the summer delicacy.

After dinner we strolled off in couples to the shore (a beach three-quarters of a mile in length), or sat under the group of trees looking on the beautiful bay.

My brother, Colonel McAllister, had exercised his engineering skill in fitting up my barn with every kind and sort of light. He improvised a chandelier for the center of it, adorned the horse and cattle stalls with vines and greens, fitted them up with seats for my guests (all nicely graveled), and put a band of music in the hay-loft, with the middle part of the barn floored over for dancing. We had a scene that Teniers has so often painted. We danced away late into the night, then had a glorious moonlight to drive home by.

I must not omit to mention one feature of these parties. It was the "Yacht Club rum punch," made from old Plantation rum, placed in huge bowls, with an immense block of ice in each bowl, the melting ice being the only liquid added to the rum, except occasionally when I would pour a bottle of champagne in, which did it no injury.

Chapter Fourteen – An Era of Great Extravagance

Let us now return to New York and its gaieties. The Assemblies were always given at Delmonico's in Fourteenth Street, the best people in the city chosen as a committee of management, and under the patronage of ladies of established position. They were large balls, and embraced all who were in what may be termed General Society. They were very enjoyable. A distinguished banker, the head of one of our old families, then gave the first *private* ball at Delmonico's to introduce his daughters to society. It was superb. The Delmonico rooms were admirably adapted for such an entertainment. There were at least eight hundred people present, and the host brought from his well-filled cellar his best Madeira and Hock. His was the pioneer private ball at this house. Being a success, it then became the fashion to give private balls at Delmonico's, and certainly one could not have found better rooms for such a purpose. One of the grandest and handsomest fancy balls ever given here was given in these rooms a little later. Absent at the South, I did not attend it. Then came in an era of great extravagance and expenditure.

A beautiful woman, who was a nightingale in song, gave a fancy ball. It was brilliantly successful, and brought its leader to the front, and gave her a large following. It made her, with the personal attractions she possessed, the belle of that winter. Among other accomplishments, she drove four horses beautifully. I remember during the summer passing her on Bellevue Avenue as she sat perched up on the box-seat of a drag, driving four fine horses, handling the ribbons with a grace and ease that was admirable. All paid court to her. She won the hearts of both men and women.

At this time a man of great energy and pluck loomed up, and attracted, in fact absorbed to a great extent, the attention of society. Full of energy and enterprise, and supplied with abundant means, he did a great deal for New York, much that will live after him. He created Jerome Park; and not only created it, but got society into it. He made it the Goodwood of America, and caused society to take an interest in it. He opened that park most brilliantly, and, by his energy and perseverance, rendered it for years a most enjoyable place for all New Yorkers. Admiring the beautiful cantatrice, he proposed to her to turn his luxurious stables into a theatre, and ask the fashionable world to come and see her act "for sweet charity's sake,"—to raise funds for the sick and wounded soldiers. In doing this, he assured her that she would literally bring the fashionable world to her feet to petition and sue for tickets of admission to this theatre. And so it proved. All flocked to see this accomplished woman act. The work of this energetic man was admirably done. He made a gem of his stable. I can but compare it to a little royal theatre. As you entered you were received by liveried servants, and by them conducted to your seat, where you found yourself surrounded by a most brilliant assemblage; and on the stage, as amateur actresses, supporting the fair singer, the fashionable beauties of that day. This was not the least of this generous man's performances. Being an admirable four-in-hand driver, he at once revived the spirit for driving four horses. He turned out daily with his drag or coach loaded with beautiful women, and drove to every desirable little country inn in and about the city, where one could dine at all well, crossing ferries, and driving up Broadway with the ease and skill of a veteran whip, which he was. His projects were, if anything, too grand. He lavished money on all these things; his conceptions were good, but, like many great minds, at times he was too unmindful of detail. On one occasion, at Newport, he came to me, and told me he had mapped out a country *fête*, asked my advice about getting it up, but failed to take it, and then brought about his first *fiasco*. He asked the *beau monde* to embark on the yachts then lying in the harbor, and go with him to Stone Bridge to a dance and clambake. All the yachtsmen placed their yachts at his disposal. At 12 M., all Newport, i.e. the fashion of the place, was on these yachts. At the prow of the boats he had placed his champagne. Down came the broiling sun, and a dead calm fell upon the waters. Tugs were called in to tow the yachts. Orders had been given that not a biscuit or glass of wine was to be served to any of the party on these boats, that we might reach the feast at the Bridge with sharp appetites. The sun went down, and the night set in before we landed. We were then taken to an orchard, the high grass a foot deep all wet, and saw before us great plates of stewed soft clams and corn that had been cooked and ready for us at 2 P.M. The women put their plates on the grass, and their feet in them, so at least to have a dry footing. The champagne was parboiled, the company enveloped in darkness, and famished, so that all pronounced this kind of clambake picnic a species of *fête* not to be indulged in knowingly a second time. The great wit of the day, his boon companion, called it "The Melancholy Fête." The following anonymous lines on this clambake were sent me:

An Adaptation of a Lamentation

Clams, clams, clams,
Will always be thrown in my teeth.
Clams, clams, clams!
I'll be crowned with a chowder wreath.

Bread and pickles and corn,
Corn and pickles and bread.
Whenever I sleep huge ghosts appear
With *clam*orous mouths to be fed.

Oh, women, with appetites strong!
Oh, girls, who I thought lived on air!
I did not mean to leave you so long
With nothing to eat, I declare.

Clams, clams, clams!
I have nothing but clams on the brain.
I'm sure all my life, and after my death
I'll be roasted and roasted again.

Oh, tugs, why could you not pull?
Oh, winds, why would you not blow?
I'm sure I did all that man could do
That my clambake shouldn't be slow.

Not in the least discouraged by this failure, returning to New York, he planned three dinners to be given by himself and two of his friends, to be the three handsomest dinners ever given in this city. Lorenzo Delmonico exclaimed, "What are the people coming to! Here, three gentlemen come to me and order three dinners, and each one charges me to make his dinner the best of the three. I am given an unlimited order, 'Charge what you will, but make my dinner the best.'" Delmonico then said to me, "I told my cook to call them the Silver, Gold, and Diamond dinners, and have novelties at them all." I attended these three dinners. Among other dishes, we had canvasback duck, cut up and made into an *aspic de canvasback*, and again, string beans, with truffles, cold, as a salad, and truffled ice cream; the last dish, strange to say, very good. At one dinner, on opening her napkin, each fair lady guest found a gold bracelet with the monogram of Jerome Park in chased gold in the centre. Now it must be remembered that this habit of giving ladies presents at dinners did not originate in this city. Before my day, the wealthy William Gaston, a bachelor, gave superb dinners in Savannah, Ga., and there, always placed at each lady's plate a beautiful Spanish fan of such value that they are preserved by the grandchildren of those ladies, and are proudly exhibited to this day.

Chapter Fifteen - On the Box Seat at Newport

It seemed at this time, that the ingenuity of man was put to the test to invent some new species of entertainment. The winter in New York being so gay, people were in the vein for frolic and amusement, and feeling rich, as the currency was inflated, prices of everything going up, Newport had a full and rushing season. The craze was for drags or coaches. My old friend, the Major, was not to be outdone, so he brought out four spanking bays; and again, an old bachelor friend of mine, a man of large fortune, but the quietest of men, I found one fine summer morning seated on the box seat of a drag, and tooling four fine roadsters. But this did not satisfy the swells. Soon came two outriders on postilion saddles, following the drag; and again, several pairs of fine horses ridden by postilions *à la demi d'Aumont*. A turnout then for a picnic was indeed an event. In those days, a beautiful spot on the water, called "The Glen," was often selected for these country parties. It was a romantic little nook, about seven miles from Newport, on what is called the East Passage, which opens on the Atlantic Ocean.

A young friend of mine, then paying court to a brilliant young woman, came to me for advice. He wanted to impress the object of his attentions, and proposed to do so by hiring two of the fastest trotting horses in Rhode Island, and driving the young lady out behind them to the "Glen" picnic. His argument was, that it was more American than any of your tandem or four-in-hands, or postilion riding; that the pace he should go at would be terrific, and he would guarantee to do the seven miles within twenty minutes. He was what we call a thorough trotting-horse man; much in love; worshipped horses; disliked style in them, going in for speed alone. I tried to dissuade him.

"It will never do," I said; "it is not the fashion; the lady you drive out will be beautifully dressed, and you will cover her with dust; besides, the pace will alarm her."

"Never fear that, my man," he answered. "The girl has grit; she will go through anything. She is none of your milk-and-water misses; I can't go too fast for her."

"Have it as you will, then," I said; and off he went to Providence to secure, through influence, these two wonderfully speedy trotters.

We were all grouped beautifully at the Glen, when, all of a sudden, we heard something descending the hill at a terrific pace; it was impossible to make out what it was, as it was completely hidden by a cloud of dust. Down it came, with lightning speed, and when it got opposite to the Major and me, we heard a loud "Whoa, my boys, whoa!" and the vehicle came to a stop. The occupants, a man and woman, were so covered with mud and dust that you could barely distinguish the one from the other. I ran up to the side of the wagon, saw a red, indignant face, and an outstretched hand imploring me to take her out. Seizing my arm, she sprang from the wagon, exclaiming, "The horrid creature! I never wish to lay eyes on him again," and then she burst into tears. Her whole light, exquisite dress was totally ruined, and she a sight to behold. Turning to him, I saw a glow of triumph in his face; his watch was in his hand. "I did it, by Jove! I did it, and ten seconds to spare!—they are tearers!"

I quietly replied, "They are indeed tearers, they have torn your business into shreds."

"Fudge, man!" he said; "she wont mind it; she was a bit scared, to be sure; but she hung on to my arm, and we came through all right." He then sought his victim. I soon saw by his dejected manner that she had given him the mitten, and, as I passed him, slowly walking his horses home, I philosophized to this extent: "Trotting horses and fashion do not combine."

Our next great day-time frolic was at Bristol Ferry. There we had a large country hotel which we took possession of. We got the best dinner giver then in Newport to lend us his *chef*, and I took my own colored cook, a native of Baltimore, who had, at the Maryland Ducking Club, gained a reputation for cooking game, ducks, etc. We determined, on this occasion, to have a trial of artistic skill between a creole woman cook, the best of her class, and the best *chef* we had in this country. We were to have sixty at dinner; dishes confined to Spanish mackerel, soft-shell crabs, woodcock, and chicken partridges. It is needless to say, the Frenchman came off victorious, though my creole cook contended that the French *chef* would not eat his own cooked dishes, but devoured her soft-shell crabs.

On this occasion we had a grand turnout of drags, postilions *à la demi d'Aumont*, and tandems. I led the cotillion myself, dancing in the large drawing-room of the inn; and it all went so charmingly that it was late into the night when we left the place. It was as dark as Erebus. We had eleven miles to drive, and I saw that some of our four-in-hand drivers felt a little squeamish. My old bachelor friend had in his drag a precious cargo. On the box-seat with him sat our nightingale, and I had in my four-seated open wagon our queen of society and a famous Baltimore belle. "Is the road straight or crooked?" I was asked, on all sides. Having danced myself nearly to death, and being well fortified with champagne, I found it straight as an arrow, as I was then oblivious to its crooks and turns. Off we all started up the hill at a canter. I remember my friend, the Major, shouting to me, "The devil take the hindmost," and the admonition to him of his old family coachman, who accompanied him that day, "Be careful, sir, the road is not as straight as it might be." Driving along at a spanking pace, the horses fresh, the ladies jubilant, I as happy as a lord,—there was a scream, then another, then a plunge, and a splash of water. Dark as it was, standing up in my wagon, I shouted, "By Jove! he has driven off the bridge,"—and off the bridge he was, drag upset and four horses mired in mud and water. One young fellow, in the excitement of the moment, sprang to the side of my wagon, and tried to wrench off one of my lamps. How then I admired the plucky, cool little woman at my side! She never lost her presence of mind for a second; gave directions quietly and effectively, and soon brought order out of chaos. From a jolly, festive procession, we were turned into a sad, melancholy species of funeral cortège. The ladies were picked out of the wreck, and placed in the different drags and wagons, and we wended on our way at a walk, ten dreary miles to Newport. One brilliant youth of the Diplomatic Corps, as we passed a farm-house, making it just out in the dark, was asked to procure for our invalids a glass of water. He rushed to the house, banging against the door, and shouting, "House, house, house, wont you hear, wont you hear?" The old farmer poked his head out of the window, answering him, "Why, man, the house can't talk! what do you want here at this time of night? I know who you are, you are some of McAllister's picnickers. I saw you go by this morning. I s'pose you want milk, but you wont get a drop here."

As picnics, country dinners, and breakfasts were then Newport's feature, they took the place of balls, all the dancing and much of the dining being done in the open air. I would here say that as every family took to these parties their butler, and carried out the wines and all the dishes, their cost in money was insignificant. We would pay twenty-five dollars for the farm or grove to which we went for the day. Twenty-five dollars for the country band, as much for the hire of silver, linen, crockery, etc., and ten dollars for a horse, wagon and man to take everything out, making the entire outlay in money on each occasion eighty-five to a hundred dollars. A picnic dinner and dance at my farm, furnishing everything myself, no outside contributions, for fifty or sixty people, would cost me then three hundred dollars, everything included. What a difference to the present time! I got up one of these country dances and luncheons summer before last at my farm, where, under a pretty grove of trees, I had built a dancing platform from which you can throw a biscuit into the beautiful waters of Narragansett Bay. Lending the farm to the party, every one bringing a dish, hiring the servants and music, cost us in money eight hundred and six dollars and eighty-four cents. There were 140 people present. The railroad running through the farm, the train stopped on the place itself within a few rods of the group of trees. Leaving Newport at 2 P.M., in six minutes we are on the place, and at a quarter of five the train returned to us, thus ridding ourselves of coachmen and grooms, finding them all at the railway station when we reached Newport on our return at 5 P.M., to take us for our usual afternoon drive.

But to return to the past. When Newport was in its glory, and outshone itself, the young men of that day resolved to give me a lesson in picnic-giving. What they had done well in and about New York, they felt they could do equally well in Newport, so they sent to the city for Delmonico with all his staff, and invited all Newport to a dance and country dinner at a large tea-house some six miles from Newport, adjoining Oaklands, the then Gibbs farm, later on the property of Mr. August Belmont, and now belonging to Mr. Cornelius Vanderbilt, being his model farm, one of the loveliest spots on Newport Island. Delmonico took possession of this huge barrack of a house, and to work his waiters went to arrange in the large, old dining-room his beautiful collation, which was all brought from New York. The entire party were dancing the cotillion in the front parlor of the house, and grouped on its front piazzas. As 5 P.M. approached, an irresistible desire, an inward craving for food, became apparent. Committeemen were beset with the question, when are we going to have the collation? They rushed off to hurry up things, and then one by one reappeared with blanched faces, and an unmistakable anxious, troubled look. Finally they came to me with, "My dear fellow, what is to be done? Come and see for yourself." Dragging me into the dining-room and pantries of the hotel I there indeed saw a sight to behold. All the coach-men and grooms had made a foray on the abundant supplies, tumbled Del-monico's French waiters into the cellar of the hotel, and locked them up; then, taking possession of the dining-room, held high carnival. Every mouth-ful of solid food was eaten up, and all the champagne drunk; the ices, jellies, and confectionery they left untouched. As I viewed the scene, I recalled Vir-gil's description of a wreck, "*Apparent rari in gurgite nantes.*" Every coach-man and groom was intoxicated, and, as the whole party at once took flight to secure dinner at home, the scene on the road beggared description. The coachmen swayed to and fro like the pendulum of a clock; the postilions of the *demi d'Aumonts* hung on by the manes of their horses, when they lost their equilibrium. The women, as usual, behaved admirably. As one said to me, "My man is beastly intoxicated, but I shall appear not to notice it. The horses are gentle, they will go of themselves." My old friend, the Major, at once held a council of war, and it was suggested that all turn in and thrash the fellows soundly, but prudence dictated that at that work man was as good as master, that the result might be doubtful; so all dolefully got away in the best manner possible. The Major thus harangued his old family coachman: "Richard, I am astonished at you; the other men's rascally conduct does not surprise me, but you, an old family servant, to so disgrace yourself, shocks me." The reply was, "I own up, Major, but indade, I am a weak craythur.

Chapter Sixteen – Social Unity

The two young women of the most distinguished bearing in my day in this country were, in my opinion, the one the daughter of our ex-Secretary of State and ex-Governor, the other the daughter of my friend, the Major. They both looked as born of noble race, and were always, when they appeared, the centre of attraction. When the engagement of the Major's daughter was announced, one of her admirers asked me to go with him to Charles Delmonico, as he was desirous of giving this fair lady a Banquet, to commemorate the initial step she had taken in woman's career. In the words of the poet, she was then

"A thought matured, but not uttered,
A conception warm and glowing, not yet embodied."

Now, all was to expand into noble womanhood, and she must needs put away childish things and bid a sweet farewell to all who had worshipped at her shrine. This worshipper wanted to make this an occasion in her life, as well as his; so with Delmonico's genius we were to conceive a banquet for this fair maid, at which, like a Queen of May, she was to sit in a bower of roses. And this she literally did, placed there by her host, a scion of one of New York's oldest families, whose family was interwoven with the Livingstons, and by marriage closely connected with the great Robert Fulton. It was the first of these lavish and gorgeous entertainments, known as Banquets. Fifty-eight guests dining in Delmonico's large ball-room; the immense oval table filling the whole room, and covered with masses of exquisite flowers. There were three fountains, one in the centre, and the others at each end of the table, throwing up a gentle spray of water, but always so planned that nothing on the table in any way impeded the sight; one from all sides of it could see over these beautiful flower-beds and through the spray. A cotillion followed the dinner, and then back all returned to the dining-room and supped as the early dawn crept on us.

Close association at a small watering-place naturally produces jars. People cannot always agree. When you become very rich and powerful, and people pay you court, it follows in many cases that you become exacting and domineering. It soon became evident that people of moderate means, who had no social power to boast of, must needs be set aside and crowded out if the one-man power, or even the united power of two or three colossally rich men, controlled society. One reflected that that would not work. The homage we pay to a society leader must come from the esteem and admiration which is felt for him, but must not be exacted or forced. It occurred then to me, that if one in any way got out with the powers that be, his position might become critical, and he so forced out of the way as to really lose his social footing. Where then was the remedy for all this? How avoid this contingency? On reflection I reached this conclusion, that in a country like ours there was always strength in union; that to blend together the solid, respectable element of any community for any project, was to create a power that would carry to success almost any enterprise; therefore, returning to New York for the winter, I looked around society and invoked the aid of the then quiet representative men of this city, to help me form an association for the purpose of giving our winter balls.

As a child, I had often listened with great interest to my father's account of his visit to London, with Dominick Lynch, the greatest swell and beau that New York had ever known. He would describe his going with this friend to Almack's, finding themselves in a brilliant assemblage of people, knowing no one, and no one deigning to notice them; Lynch, turning to my father, exclaimed: "Well, my friend, geese indeed were we to thrust ourselves in here where we are evidently not wanted." He had hardly finished the sentence, when the Duke of Wellington (to whom they had brought letters, and who had sent them tickets to Almack's) entered, looked around, and, seeing them, at once approached them, took each by the arm, and walked them twice up and down the room; then, pleading an engagement, said "good-night" and left. Their countenances fell as he rapidly left the room, but the door had barely closed on him, when all crowded around them, and in a few minutes they were presented to every one of note, and had a charming evening. He described to us how Almack's originated,—all by the banding together of powerful women of influence for the purpose of getting up these balls, and in this way making them the greatest social events of London society.

Remembering all this, I resolved in 1872 to establish in New York an American Almack's, taking men instead of women, being careful to select only the leading representative men of the city, who had the right to create and lead society. I knew all would depend upon our making a proper selection.

There is one rule in life I invariably carry out—never to rely wholly on my own judgment, but to get the advice of others, weigh it well and satisfy myself of its correctness, and then act on it. I went in this city to those who could make the best analysis of men; who knew their past as well as their present, and could foresee their future. In this way, I made up an Executive Committee of three gentlemen, who daily met at my house, and we went to work in earnest to make a list of those we should ask to join in the undertaking. One of this Committee, a very bright, clever man, hit upon the name of Patriarchs for the Association, which was at once adopted, and then, after some discussion, we limited the number of Patriarchs to twenty-five, and that each Patriarch, for his subscription, should have the right of inviting to each ball four ladies and five gentlemen, including himself and family; that all distinguished

strangers, up to fifty, should be asked; and then established the rules govern-
ing the giving of these balls—all of which, with some slight modifications,
have been carried out to the letter to this day. The following gentlemen were
then asked to become "Patriarchs," and at once joined the little band:

JOHN JACOB ASTOR,	ROYAL PHELPS,
WILLIAM ASTOR,	EDWIN A. POST,
DE LANCEY KANE,	A. GRACIE KING,
WARD MCALLISTER,	LEWIS M. RUTHERFORD,
GEORGE HENRY WARREN,	ROBERT G. REMSEN,
EUGENE A. LIVINGSTON,	WM. C. SCHERMERHORN,
WILLIAM BUTLER DUNCAN,	FRANCIS R. RIVES,
E. TEMPLETON SNELLING,	MATURIN LIVINGSTON,
LEWIS COLFORD JONES,	ALEX. VAN RENSSELAER,
JOHN W. HAMERSLEY,	WALTER LANGDON,
BENJAMIN S. WELLES,	F. G. D'HAUTEVILLE,
FREDERICK SHELDON,	C. C. GOODHUE,

WILLIAM R. TRAVERS.

The object we had in view was to make these balls thoroughly representative; to embrace the old Colonial New Yorkers, our adopted citizens, and men
whose ability and integrity had won the esteem of the community, and who
formed an important element in society. We wanted the money power, but
not in any way to be controlled by it. Patriarchs were chosen solely for their
fitness; on each of them promising to invite to each ball only such people as
would do credit to the ball. We then resolved that the responsibility of inviting each batch of nine guests should rest upon the shoulders of the Patriarch
who invited them, and that if any objectionable element was introduced, it
was the Management's duty to at once let it be known by whom such objectionable party was invited, and to notify the Patriarch so offending, that he
had done us an injury, and pray him to be more circumspect. He then stood
before the community as a sponsor of his guest, and all society, knowing the
offense he had committed, would so upbraid him, that he would go and sin
no more. We knew then, and we know now, that the whole secret of the success of these Patriarch Balls lay in making them select; in making them the
most brilliant balls of each winter; in making it extremely difficult to obtain
an invitation to them, and to make such invitations of great value; to make
them the stepping-stone to the best New York society, that one might be sure
that any one repeatedly invited to them had a secure social position, and to
make them the best managed, the best looked-after balls given in this city. I
soon became as much interested in them as if I were giving them in my own
house; their success I felt was my success, and their failure, my failure; and
be assured, this identifying oneself with any undertaking is the secret of its
success. One should never say, "Oh, it is a subscription ball; I'm not responsi-
ble for it." It must always be said, "I must be more careful in doing this for

others, than in doing it for myself." Nothing must be kept in view but the great result to be reached, i.e. the success of the entertainment, the pleasure of the whole. When petitioned to curtail the expense, lower the subscription, our reply has always been, "We cannot do it if it endangers the success of the balls. While we give them, let us make them the great social events in New York society; make our suppers the best that can be given in this city; decorate our rooms as lavishly as good taste permits, spare no expense to make them a credit to ourselves and to the great city in which they are given."

The social life of a great part of our community, in my opinion, hinges on this and similar organizations, for it and they are organized social power, capable of giving a passport to society to all worthy of it. We thought it would not be wise to allow a handful of men having royal fortunes to have a sovereign's prerogative, i.e. to say whom society shall receive, and whom society shall shut out. We thought it better to try and place such power in the hands of representative men, the choice falling on them solely because of their worth, respectability, and responsibility.

Chapter Seventeen – A Golden Age of Feasting

As a rule, in this city, heads of families came to the front, and took an active part in society when they wished to introduce their daughters into it.

The first Patriarch Balls were given in the winters of 1872 and 1873. At this period, a great personage (representing a silent power that had always been recognized and felt in this community, so long as I remember, by not only fashionable people, but by the solid old quiet element as well) had daughters to introduce into society, which brought her prominently forward and caused her at once to take a leading position. She possessed great administrative power, and it was soon put to good use and felt by society. I then, for the first time, was brought in contact with this *grande dame*, and at once recognized her ability, and felt that she would become society's leader, and that she was admirably qualified for the position.

It was not long before circumstances forced her to assume the leadership, which she did, and which she has held with marked ability ever since, having all the qualities necessary,—good judgment and a great power of analysis of men and women, a thorough knowledge of all their surroundings, a just appreciation of the rights of others, and, coming herself from an old Colonial family, a good appreciation of the value of ancestry; always keeping it near her, and bringing it in, in all social matters, but also understanding the importance and power of the new element; recognizing it, and fairly and generously awarding to it a prominent place. Having a great fortune, she had the ability to conceive and carry out social projects; and this she has done, always with success, ever ready to recognize ability and worth, and give to it advice and assistance. Above all things, a true and loyal friend in sunshine or shower. Deeply interested in the welfare of this city, she lent herself to any undertaking she felt worthy of her support, and once promising it her aid, she could be always relied on and always found most willing to advance its interests. With such a friend, we felt the Patriarchs had an additional social strength that would give them the solidity and lasting powers which they have shown they possess. Whenever we required advice and assistance on or about them, we went to her, and always found ourselves rewarded in so doing by receiving suggestions that were invaluable. Quick to criticise any defect of lighting or ornamentation, or arrangement, she was not backward in chiding the management for it, and in this way made these balls what they were in the past, what they are in the present, and what we hope they may be in the future.

The Patriarchs, from their very birth, became a great social feature. You could but read the list of those who gave these balls, to see at a glance that they embraced not only the smart set, but the old Knickerbocker families as well; and that they would, from the very nature of the case, representing the best society of this great commercial city, have to grow and enlarge. Applications to be made Patriarchs poured in from all sides; every influence was brought to bear to secure a place in this little band, and the pressure was so great that we feared the struggle would be too fierce and engender too much rancor and bad feeling, and that this might of itself destroy them. The argument against them, the one most strongly urged, was that they were overturning all old customs; that New Yorkers had been in the habit of taking an active part in society only when they had daughters to bring out, *lancée-ing* their daughters, and they themselves taking a back seat. But that here in this new association, the married women took a more prominent place than the young girls; *they* were the belles of the balls, and not the young girls. This was Europeanizing New York too rapidly.

Hearing all this, and fearing we would grow unpopular, to satisfy the public we at once got up a new association, wholly for the young girls, and called it The Family Circle Dancing Class. Its name would in itself explain what it was, a small gathering of people in a very small and intimate way, so that unless one was in close intimacy with those getting up these dances, they would have no possible claim to be included in them. Any number of small subscription parties had been formed, such as "The Ancient and Honorables," "The New and Notables," "The Mysterious," and "The Fortnightlies." All had been most enjoyable, but short-lived. The F. C. D. C's. were to be, in fact, "Junior Patriarchs," under the same management, and were to be cherished and nourished by the same organization. They were given at first in six private houses. The first was held at Mr. William Butler Duncan's; the second at Mr. Ward McAllister's; the third at Mr. De Lancey Kane's; the fourth at Mr. William Astor's; the fifth at Mr. George Henry Warren's, and the sixth at Mr. Lewis Colford Jones's. I gave mine in my house in West Nineteenth Street, and then saw what it was to turn a house inside out for a ball, and how contracted everything must necessarily be in a twenty-five foot house, to receive

guests in it, give them a *salle de danse* and a supper room, and then concluded that we must go in most cases to a good-sized ball-room to give an enjoyable dance.

From the first, these dances were very popular. They gave the Patriarch
balls the relief they required, and were rapidly growing in favor and threatened in the end to become formidable rivals of the Patriarchs. The same
pains were taken in getting them up, as were given to the Patriarchs. We had
them but for one season in private houses, and then gave them at Dod-
worth's, now Delmonico's. Later on, when this house changed hands and became Delmonico's, we gave them all there, with the exception of one winter
when we gave them in the foyers of the Metropolitan Opera House. We made
the subscription to them an individual subscription, each lady and gentleman
subscribing $12.00 for the three balls. One of them at Delmonico's we made a
"Mother Goose" Ball. It was a species of fancy dress ball, powdered hair being *de rigueur* for all ladies who did not wear fancy costumes, and the feature
of the occasion was the "Mother Goose" Quadrille, which had been planned
and prepared with much skill and taste. This Quadrille was made up of sixteen couples and was danced at eleven o'clock. As those who danced in it
passed you as they marched from the hall into the ball-room, you found it a
beautiful sight truly. Many of the men wore pink. Some of the characters
were droll indeed. Among others, "Tom, Tom, the Piper's son," with his tradi-
tional pig; "A man in the moon, who had come down too soon"; one lady as
"Twinkle, twinkle, little star"; "Mother Hubbard," in an artistic costume of
scarlet chintz; "Mary, Mary, quite contrary"; "Little Bo-Peep," "The Maid in
the garden hanging out the clothes," "Punch and Judy"; "Oranges and Lem-
ons"; while M. de Talleyrand appeared as a *mignon* of Henry the Second.
"Mother Goose" herself was also there. The feature of the evening was the
singing of the nursery rhymes. The second was the "Pinafore" Quadrille introducing the music of that operetta. All the men who danced in it were in
sailor's dress. Then followed a Hunting Quadrille, in which every man wore a
scarlet coat.

I little knew what I was undertaking when I started these F. C. D. C. Balls.
From the giving of the first of these dances, out of a private house, to the time
of my giving them up, I had no peace either at home or abroad. I was assailed
on all sides, became in a sense a diplomat, committed myself to nothing,
promised much and performed as little as possible. I saw at once the rock on
which we must split: that the pressure would be so great to get in, no one
could resist it; that our parties must become too general, and that in the end
the smart set would give up going to them. I knew that when this occurred,
they were doomed; but I fought for their existence manfully, and if I could
here narrate all I went through to keep these small parties select, I would fill
a volume. My mornings were given up to being interviewed of and about
them; mothers would call at my house, entirely unknown to me, the sole
words of introduction being, "Kind sir, I have a daughter." These words were
cabalistic; I would spring up, bow to the ground, and reply: "My dear madam,

say no more, you have my sympathy; we are in accord; no introduction is necessary; you have a daughter, and want her to go to the F. C. D. C's. I will do all in my power to accomplish this for you; but my dear lady, please understand, that in all matters concerning these little dances I must consult the powers that be. I am their humble servant; I must take orders from them." All of which was a figure of speech on my part. "May I ask if you know any one in this great city, and whom do you know? for to propitiate the powers that be, I must be able to give them some account of your daughter." This was enough to set my fair visitor off. The family always went back to King John, and in some instances to William the Conqueror. "My dear madam," I would reply, "does it not satisfy any one to come into existence with the birth of one's country? In my opinion, four generations of gentlemen make as good and true a gentleman as forty. I know my English brethren will not agree with me in this, but, in spite of them, it is my belief." With disdain, my fair visitor would reply, "You are easily satisfied, sir." And so on, from day to day, these interviews would go on; all were Huguenots, Pilgrims, or Puritans. I would sometimes call one a Pilgrim in place of a Puritan, and by this would uncork the vials of wrath. If they had ever lived south of Mason and Dixon's line, their ancestor was always a near relative of Washington, or a Fairfax, or of the "first families of Virginia." Others were more frank, and claimed no ancestry, but simply wished to know "how the thing was to be done." When our list was full, all comers were told this, but this did not stop them. I was then daily solicited and prayed to give them the first vacancy. I did the best in my power, found out who people were, and if it was possible asked them to join.

The little dances were most successful. Year by year they improved. They were handsomer each season. We were not content with the small buffet in the upper ball-room at Delmonico's, but supped, as did the Patriarchs, in the large room on Fifth Avenue and Twenty-sixth Street, and literally had equally as good suppers, leaving out terrapin and canvasback. But when the ladies organized Assembly Balls, we then thought that there would perhaps be too many subscription balls, and the F. C. D. C. was given up.

At this time, when the F. C. D. C.'s were in high favor, I received the following amusing anonymous lines of and about them:

> He does not reign in Russia cold,
> Nor yet in far Cathay,
> But o'er this town he's come to hold
> An undisputed sway.
>
> When in their might the ladies rose,
> "To put the Despot down,"
> As blandly as Ah Sin, he goes
> His way without a frown.
> Alas! though he's but one alone,
> He's one too many still—

He's fought the fight, he's held his own,
And to the end he will.

—*From a Lady after the Ball of 25th February, 1884.*

Just at this time a man of wealth, who had accumulated a fortune here, re-solved to give New Yorkers a sensation; to give them a banquet which should exceed in luxury and expense anything before seen in this country. As he ex-pressed it, "I knew it would be a folly, a piece of unheard-of extravagance, but as the United States Government had just refunded me $10,000, exacted from me for duties upon importations (which, being excessive, I had peti-tioned to be returned me, and had quite unexpectedly received this sum back), I resolved to appropriate it to giving a banquet that would always be remembered." Accordingly, he went to Charles Delmonico, who in turn went to his *cuisine classique* to see how they could possibly spend this sum on this feast. Success crowned their efforts. The sum in such skillful hands soon melted away, and a banquet was given of such beauty and magnificence, that even New Yorkers, accustomed as they were to every species of novel ex-penditure, were astonished at its lavishness, its luxury. The banquet was giv-en at Delmonico's, in Fourteenth Street. There were seventy-two guests in the large ball-room, looking on Fifth Avenue. The table covered the whole length and breadth of the room, only leaving a passageway for the waiters to pass around it. It was a long extended oval table, and every inch of it was covered with flowers, excepting a space in the centre, left for a lake, and a border around the table for the plates. This lake was indeed a work of art; it was an oval pond, thirty feet in length, by nearly the width of the table, in-closed by a delicate golden wire network, reaching from table to ceiling, mak-ing the whole one grand cage; four superb swans, brought from Prospect Park, swam in it, surrounded by high banks of flowers of every species and variety, which prevented them from splashing the water on the table. There were hills and dale; the modest little violet carpeting the valleys, and other bolder sorts climbing up and covering the tops of those miniature mountains. Then, all around the inclosure, and in fact above the entire table, hung little golden cages, with fine songsters, who filled the room with their melody, oc-casionally interrupted by the splashing of the waters of the lake by the swans, and the cooing of these noble birds, and at one time by a fierce com-bat between these stately, graceful, gliding white creatures. The surface of the whole table, by clever art, was one unbroken series of undulations, rising and falling like the billows of the sea, but all clothed and carpeted with every form of blossom. It seemed like the abode of fairies; and when surrounding this fairyland with lovely young American womanhood, you had indeed an unequaled scene of enchantment. But this was not to be alone a feast for the eye; all that art could do, all that the cleverest men could devise to spread before the guests, such a feast as the gods should enjoy, was done, and so well done that all present felt, in the way of feasting, that man could do no more! The wines were perfect. Blue seal Johannisberg flowed like water. Incomparable '48 claret, superb Burgundies, and amber-colored Madeira, all were there to add to the intoxicating delight of the scene. Then, soft music stole over one's senses; lovely women's eyes sparkled with delight at the beauty of their surroundings, and I felt that the fair being who sat next to me would have graced Alexander's feast

"Sitting by my side,
  Like a lovely Eastern bride,
  In flower of youth and beauty's pride."

Chapter Eighteen – Entering Society

I would now make some suggestions as to the proper way of introducing a young girl into New York society, particularly if she is not well supported by an old family connection. It is cruel to take a girl to a ball where she knows no one,

"And to subject her to
  The fashionable stare of twenty score
  Of well-bred persons, called the world."

Had I charged a fee for every consultation with anxious mothers on this subject, I would be a rich man. I well remember a near relative of mine once writing me from Paris, as follows: "I consign my wife and daughter to your care. They will spend the winter in New York; at once give them a ball at Delmonico's, and draw on me for the outlay." I replied, "My dear fellow, how many people do you know in this city whom you could invite to a ball? The funds you send me will be used, but not in giving a ball." The girl being a beauty, all the rest was easy enough. I gave her theatre party after theatre party, followed by charming little suppers, asked to them the *jeunesse dorée* of the day; took her repeatedly to the opera, and saw that she was there always surrounded by admirers; incessantly talked of her fascinations; assured my young friends that she was endowed with a fortune equal to the mines of Ophir, that she danced like a dream, and possessed all the graces, a sunbeam across one's path; then saw to it that she had a prominent place in every cotillion, and a fitting partner; showed her whom to smile upon, and on whom to frown; gave her the *entrée* to all the nice houses; criticised severely her toilet until it became perfect; daily met her on the Avenue with the most charming man in town, who by one pretext or another I turned over to her; made her the constant subject of conversation; insisted upon it that she was to be the belle of the coming winter; advised her parents that she should have her first season at Bar Harbor, where she could learn to flirt to her heart's content, and vie with other girls. Her second summer, when she was older, I suggested her passing at Newport, where she should have a pair of ponies, a pretty trap, with a well-gotten-up groom, and Worth to dress her. Here I hinted that much must depend on her father's purse, as to her wardrobe. As a friend of mine once said to me, "Your pace is charming, but can you keep it up?" I also advised keeping the young girl well in hand and not letting her give offense to the powers that be; to see to it that she was not the first to arrive and the last to leave a ball, and further, that nothing was more winning in a girl than a pleasant bow and a gracious smile given to either young or old. The fashion now for women is to hold themselves erect. The modern manner of shaking hands I do not like, but yet it is adopted. Being interested in the girl's success, I further impressed upon her the importance of making herself agreeable to older people, remembering that much of her enjoyment would be derived from them. If asked to dance a cotillion, let it be conditional that no bouquet be sent her; to be cautious how she refused the first offers of marriage made her, as they were generally the best.

A word, just here, to the newly married. It works well to have the man more in love with you than you are with him. My advice to all young married women is to keep up flirting with their husbands as much after marriage as before; to make themselves as attractive to their husbands after their marriage as they were when they captivated them; not to neglect their toilet, but rather improve it; to be as coquettish and coy after they are bound together as before, when no ties held them. The more they are appreciated by the world, the more will their husbands value them. In fashionable life, conspicuous jealousy is a mistake. A woman is bound to take and hold a high social position. In this way she advances and strengthens her husband. How many women we see who have benefited their husbands, and secured for them these advantages.

A young girl should be treated like a bride when she makes her *débût* into society. Her relatives should rally around her and give her entertainments to welcome her into the world which she is to adorn. It is in excessive bad taste for such relatives to in any way refer to the cost of these dinners, balls, etc. Every one in society knows how to estimate such things. Again, at such dinners, it is not in good taste to load your table with *bonbonnières* and other articles intended to be taken away by your guests. This reminds me of a dear old lady, who, when I dined with her, always insisted on my putting in my dress coat pocket a large hothouse peach, which never reached home in a perfect state.

The launching of a beautiful young girl into society is one thing; it is another to place her family on a good, sound social footing. You can launch them into the social sea, but can they float? "Manners maketh man," is an old proverb. These they certainly must possess. There is no society in the world as generous as New York society is; "friend, parent, neighbor, all it will embrace," but once embraced they must have the power of sustaining themselves. The best quality for them to possess is modesty in asserting their claims; letting people seek them rather than attempting to rush too quickly to the front. The Prince of Wales, on a charming American young woman expressing her surprise at the cordial reception given her by London society, replied, "My dear lady, there are certain people who are bound to come to the front and stay there; you are one of them." It requires not only money, but brains, and, above all, infinite tact; possessing the three, your success is assured. If taken by the hand by a person in society you are at once led into the charmed circle, and then your own correct perceptions of what should or should not be done must do the rest. As a philosophical friend once said to me, "A gentleman can always walk, but he cannot afford to have a shabby equipage." Another philosopher soliloquized as follows: "The first evidence of wealth is your equipage." By the way, his definition of aristocracy in America was, the possession of hereditary wealth.

If you want to be fashionable, be always in the company of fashionable people. As an old beau suggested to me, If you see a fossil of a man, shabbily dressed, relying solely on his pedigree, dating back to time immemorial, who has the aspirations of a duke and the fortunes of a footman, do not cut him; it is better to cross the street and avoid meeting him. It is well to be in with the nobs who are born to their position, but the support of the swells is more advantageous, for society is sustained and carried on by the swells, the nobs looking quietly on and accepting the position, feeling they are there by divine right; but they do not make fashionable society, or carry it on. A nob can be a swell if he chooses, i.e. if he will spend the money; but for his social existence this is unnecessary. A nob is like a poet,—*nascitur non fit*; not so a swell,—he creates himself.

The value of a pleasant manner it is impossible to estimate. It is like sunshine, it gladdens; you feel it and are at once attracted to the person without knowing why. When you entertain, do it in an easy, natural way, as if it was an everyday occurrence, not the event of your life; but do it well. Learn how to do it; never be ashamed to learn. The American people have a *greater* power of "catching hold," and adapting themselves to new surroundings than any other people in the world. A distinguished diplomatist once said to me, "The best wife for a Diplomat is an American; for take her to any quarter of the globe and she adapts herself to the place and people."

If women should cultivate pleasant manners, should not men do the same? Are not manners as important to men as to women? The word "gentleman" may have its derivation from gentle descent, but my understanding of a gentleman has always been that he is a person free from arrogance, and anything like self-assertion; considerate of the feelings of others; so satisfied and secure in his own position, that he is always unpretentious, feeling he could not do an ungentlemanly act; as courteous and kind in manner to his inferiors as to his equals. The best bred men I have ever met have always been the least pretentious. Natural and simple in manner, modest in apparel, never wearing anything too *voyant*, or conspicuous; but always so well dressed that you could never discover what made them so,—the good, quiet taste of the whole producing the result.

Here, all men are more or less in business. We hardly have a class who are not. They are, of necessity, daily brought in contact with all sorts and conditions of men, and in self-defense oftentimes have to acquire and adopt an abrupt, a brusque manner of address, which, as a rule, they generally leave in their offices when they quit them. If they do not, they certainly should. When such rough manners become by practice a second nature, they unfit one to go into society. It pays well for young and old to cultivate politeness and courtesy. Nothing is gained by trying roughly to elbow yourself into society, and push your way through into the inner circle; for when such a one has reached it, he will find its atmosphere uncongenial and be only too glad to escape from it.

A short time ago, a handsome, well-dressed Englishman, well up in all matters pertaining to society, went with me to my tailor to see me try on a dress coat. I was struck with his criticisms. Standing before a glass, he said, "You must never be able to see the tails of your dress coat; if you do, discard the coat." Again, he advised one's always wearing a hat that was the fashion, losing sight of the becoming, but always following the fashion. "At a glance," he said, "I can tell a man from the provinces, simply by his hat." If you are stout, never wear a white waistcoat, or a conspicuous watch-chain. Never call attention by them to what you should try to conceal. In going to the opera, if you go to an opera box with ladies, you should wear white or light French gray gloves. Otherwise, gloves are not worn. A *boutonnière* of white hyacinths or white pinks on dress coats is much worn, both to balls and the opera. My English friend was very much struck with the fact that American women all sat on the left side of the carriage, the opposite side from what they do in England. "Ladies," he said, "should always sit behind their coachman, but the desire to see and be seen prompts them here to take the other side. In this city some half a dozen ladies show their knowledge of conventionalities and take the proper seat."

I think the great secret of life is to be contented with the position to which it has pleased God to call you. Living myself in a modest, though comfortable little house in Twenty-first Street in this city, a Wall Street banker honored me with a visit, and exclaimed against my surroundings.

"What!" said he, "are you contented to live in this modest little house? Why, man, this will never do! The first thing you must have is a fine house. I will see that you get it. All that you have to do is to let me buy ten thousand shares of stock for you at the opening of the Board; by three I can sell it, and I will then send you a check for the profit of the transaction, which will not be less than ten thousand dollars! Do it for you? Of course I will, with pleasure. You will run no risk; if there is a loss I will bear it."

I thanked my friend, assured him I was wholly and absolutely contented, and must respectfully decline his offer. A similar offer was made to me by my old friend, Commodore Vanderbilt, in his house in Washington Place. I was a great admirer of this grand old man, and he was very fond of me. He had taken me over his stables, and was then showing me his parlors and statuary, and kept all the time calling me "his boy." I turned to him and said, "Commodore, you will be as great a railroad king, as you were once an ocean king, and as you call me your boy, why don't you make my fortune?" He thought a moment, and then said, slapping me on the back, "Mc, sell everything you have and put it in Harlem stock; it is now twenty-four; you will make more money than you will know how to take care of." If I had followed his advice, I would now have been indeed a millionaire.

One word more here about the Commodore. He then turned to me and said, "Mc, look at that bust,"—a bust of himself, by Powers. "What do you think Powers said of that head?"

"What did he say?" I replied.

"He said, 'It is a finer head than Webster's!'"

Chapter Nineteen - Entertaining

"We may live without love,—what is passion but pining?
But where is the man who can live without dining?"
— Owen Meredith.

The first object to be aimed at is to make your dinners so charming and agreeable that invitations to them are eagerly sought for, and to let all feel that it is a great privilege to dine at your house, where they are sure they will meet only those whom they wish to meet. You cannot instruct people by a book how to entertain, though Aristotle is said to have applied *his* talents to a compilation of a code of laws for the table. Success in entertaining is accomplished by magnetism and tact, which combined constitute social genius. It is the ladder to social success. If successfully done, it naturally creates jealousy. I have known a family who for years outdid every one in giving exquisite dinners—(this was when this city was a small community)—driven to Europe and passing the rest of their days there on finding a neighbor outdoing them. I myself once lost a charming friend by giving a better soup than he did. His wife rushed home from my house, and in despair, throwing up her hands to her husband, exclaimed, "Oh! what a soup!" I related this to my cousin, the distinguished *gourmet*, who laughingly said: "Why did you not at once invite them to pork and beans?"

The highest cultivation in social manners enables a person to conceal from the world his real feelings. He can go through any annoyance as if it were a pleasure; go to a rival's house as if to a dear friend's; "Smile and smile, yet murder while he smiles." A great compliment once paid me in Newport was the speech of an old public waiter, who had grown gray in the service, when to a *confrère* he exclaimed: "In this house, my friend, you meet none but quality."

In planning a dinner the question is not to whom you owe dinners, but who is most desirable. The success of the dinner depends as much upon the company as the cook. Discordant elements—people invited alphabetically, or to pay off debts—are fatal. Of course, I speak of ladies' dinners. And here, great tact must be used in bringing together young womanhood and the dowagers. A dinner wholly made up of young people is generally stupid. You require the experienced woman of the world, who has at her fingers' ends the history of past, present, and future. Critical, scandalous, with keen and ready wit, appreciating the dinner and wine at their worth. Ladies in beautiful toilets are necessary to the elegance of a dinner, as a most exquisitely arranged table is only a solemn affair surrounded by black coats. I make it a rule never to attend such dismal feasts, listening to prepared witticisms and "twice-told tales." So much for your guests.

The next step is an interview with your *chef*, if you have one, or *cordon bleu*, whom you must arouse to fever heat by working on his ambition and vanity. You must impress upon him that this particular dinner will give him fame and lead to fortune. My distinguished cousin, who enjoyed the reputation of being one of the most finished *gourmets* in this country, when he reached this point, would bury his head in his hands and (seemingly to the *chef*) rack his brain seeking inspiration, fearing lest the fatal mistake should occur of letting two white or brown sauces follow each other in succession; or truffles appear twice in that dinner. The distress that his countenance wore as he repeatedly looked up at the *chef*, as if for advice and assistance, would have its intended effect on the culinary artist, and *his* brain would at once act in sympathy.

The first battle is over the soup, and here there is a vast difference of opinion. In this country, where our servants are oftentimes unskilled, and have a charming habit of occasionally giving ladies a soup shower bath, I invariably discard two soups, and insist to the protesting *chef* that there shall be but one. Of course, if there are two, the one is light, the other heavy. Fortunately for the period in which we live, our great French artists have invented the *Tortue claire*; which takes the place of our forefathers' Mock Turtle soup, with forcemeat balls, well spiced, requiring an ostrich's digestion to survive it. We have this, then, as our soup. The *chef* here exclaims, "Monsieur must know that all *petites bouchées* must, of necessity, be made of chicken." We ask for a novelty, and his great genius suggests, under pressure, *mousse aux jambon*, which is attractive to the eye, and, if well made, at once establishes the reputation of the artist, satisfies the guests that they are in able hands, and allays their fears for their dinner.

There is but one season of the year when salmon should be served hot at a choice repast; that is in the spring and early summer, and even then it is too satisfying, not sufficiently delicate. The man who gives salmon during the winter, I care not what sauce he serves with it, does an injury to himself and his guests. Terrapin is with us as national a dish as canvasback, and at the choicest dinners is often a substitute for fish. It is a shellfish, and an admirable change from the oft repeated *filet de sole* or *filet de bass*. At the South, terrapin soup, with plenty of eggs in it, was a dish for the gods, and a standard dinner party dish in days when a Charleston and Savannah dinner was an event to live for. But no Frenchman ever made this soup. It requires the native born culinary genius of the African.

Now when we mention the word terrapin, we approach a very delicate subject, involving a rivalry between two great cities; a subject that has been agitated for thirty years or more, and is still agitated, i.e. the proper way of cooking terrapin. The Baltimoreans contending that the black stew, the chafing dish system, simply adding to the terrapin salt, pepper, and Madeira, produce the best dish; while the Philadelphians contend that by fresh butter and cream they secure greater results. The one is known as the Baltimore black stew; the other, as the Trenton stew, this manner of cooking terrapin originating in an old eating club in Trenton, N. J. I must say I agree with the Philadelphians.

And now, leaving the fish, we come to the *pièce de resistance* of the dinner, called the *relévé*. No Frenchman will ever willingly cook a ladies' dinner and give anything coarser or heavier than a *filet de bœuf*. He will do it, if he has to, of course, but he will think you a barbarian if you order him to do it. I eschew the mushroom and confine myself to the truffle in the treatment of the *filet*. I oftentimes have a *filet à la mœlle de bœuf*, or *à la jardinière*. In the fall of the year, turkey *poults à la Bordelaise*, or *à la Toulouse*, or a saddle of Southdown mutton or lamb, are a good substitute. Let me here say that the American turkey, as found on Newport Island, all its feathers being jet black and its diet grasshoppers, is exceptionally fine.

Now for the *entrées*. In a dinner of twelve or fourteen, one or two hot *entrées* and one cold is sufficient. If you use the truffle with the *filet*, making a black sauce, you must follow it with a white sauce, as a *riz de veau à la Toulouse*, or a *suprême de volaille*; then a *chaud-froid*, say of *pâté de foie gras en Bellevue*, which simply means *pâté de foie gras* incased in jelly. Then a hot vegetable, as artichokes, sauce *Barigoule*, or *Italienne*, or asparagus, sauce *Hollandaise*. Then your *sorbet*, known in France as *la surprise*, as it is an ice, and produces on the mind the effect that the dinner is finished, when the grandest dish of the dinner makes its appearance in the shape of the roast canvasbacks, woodcock, snipe, or truffled capons, with salad.

I must be permitted a few words of and about this *sorbet*. It should never be flavored with rum. A true Parisian *sorbet* is simply "*punch à la Toscane*," flavored with *Maraschino* or bitter almonds; in other words, a homœopathic dose of prussic acid. Then the *sorbet* is a digestive, and is intended as such. *Granit*, or water ice, flavored with rum, is universally given here. Instead of aiding digestion, it impedes it, and may be dangerous.

A Russian salad is a pleasing novelty at times, and is more attractive if it comes in the shape of a *Macedoine de legumes*, Camembert cheese, with a biscuit, with which you serve your Burgundy, your old Port, or your Johannisberg, the only place in the dinner where you can introduce this latter wine. A genuine Johannisberg, I may say here, by way of parenthesis, is rare in this country, for if obtained at the Chateau, it is comparatively a dry wine; if it is, as I have often seen it, still lusciously sweet after having been here twenty years or more, you may be sure it is not a genuine Chateau wine.

The French always give a hot pudding, as pudding *suedoise*, or a *croute au Madère*, or *ananas*, but I always omit this dish to shorten the dinner. Then come your ices. The fashion now is to make them very ornamental, a *cornucopia* for instance, but I prefer a *pouding Nesselrode*, the best of all the ices if good cream is used.

Chapter Twenty - Madeiras

Having had your champagne from the fish to the roast, your *vin ordinaire* through the dinner, your Burgundy or Johannisberg, or fine old Tokay (quite equal to any Johannisberg), with the cheese, your best claret with the roast, then after the ladies have had their fruit and have left the table, comes on the king of wines, your Madeira; a national wine, a wine only well matured at the South, and a wine whose history is as old as is that of our country. I may here say, that Madeira imparts a vitality that no other wine can give. After drinking it, it acts as a soporific, but the next day you feel ten years younger and stronger for it. I have known a man, whose dinners were so famous by reason of his being always able to give at them a faultless Madeira, disappear with his wine. When his wine gave out, he collapsed. When asked, "Where is Mr. Jones?" the ready answer was always given, "He went out with his 'Rapid' Madeira."

Families prided themselves on their Madeira. It became an heirloom (as Tokay now is, in Austria). Like the elephant, it seemed to live over three score years and ten. The fine Madeiras were fine when they reached this country. Age improved them, and made them the poetry of wine. They became the color of amber and retained all their original flavor. But it is an error to suppose that age ever improved a poor Madeira. If it came here poor and sweet, it remained poor and sweet, and never lost its sweetness, even at seventy or eighty years, while the famous Madeiras, dating as far back as 1791, if they have been properly cared for, are perfect to this day. We should value wine like women, for maturity, not age.

These wines took their names generally from the ships in which they came over. There is no more sensitive wine to climatic influences. A delicate Madeira, taken only a few blocks on a cold, raw day, is not fit to drink; and again, you might as well give a man champagne out of a horse bucket, as to give him a Madeira in a thick sherry or claret glass, or a heavy cut glass. The American pipe-stem is the only glass in which Madeira should be given, and when thus given, is, as one of our distinguished men once said, "The only liquid he ever called wine." This ought to be given as was done by the Father of the Roman

71

Lucullus, who never saw more than a single cup of the Phanean wine served at one time at his father's table.

A friend of mine once gave the proprietor of the Astor House, for courtesies extended to him, a dozen of his finest Madeira. He had the curiosity years after to ask his host of the Astor what became of this wine. He replied, "Daniel Webster came to my house, and I opened a bottle of it for him, and he remained in the house until he had drunk up every drop of it." This was the famous "Butler 16."

As in painting there are the Murillo and Correggio schools, the light ethereal conceptions of womanhood, as against the rich Titian coloring; so in Madeira, there is the full, round, strong, rich wine, liked by some in preference to the light, delicate, straw-colored, rain-water wines. Philadelphians first took to this character of wine. They judiciously "fined" their wine, and produced simply a perfect Madeira,—to be likened to the best Johannisberg, and naturally so, it having similar qualities, as it is well known that the Sercial Madeira, the "king pin" of all Madeiras, was raised from a Rhine grape taken to the Island of Madeira. And here let me say, that "fining," by using only the white of a perfectly fresh egg and Spanish clay, is proper and judicious, but milk is ruinous. The eggs in Spain are famous, and are thus used.

In Savannah and Charleston, from 1800 up to our Civil War, afternoon wine parties were the custom. You were asked to come and taste Madeira, at 5 P.M., *after your dinner*. The hour of dining in these cities was then always 3 P.M. The mahogany table, which reflected your face, was set with finger bowls, with four pipe-stem glasses in each bowl, olives, parched ground nuts and almonds, and half a dozen bottles of Madeira. There you sat, tasted and commented on these wines for an hour or more. On one occasion, a gentleman, not having any wine handy, mixed half "Catherine Banks" and half "Rapid." On tasting the mixture, a great wine expert said if he could believe his host capable of mixing a wine, he would say it was "half Catherine Banks and half Rapid." This was after fifteen men had said they could not name the Madeira.

A distinguished stranger having received an invitation to one of these wine parties from the British Consul, replied, "Thanks, I must decline, for where I dine I take my wine."

The oldest and largest shippers of Madeira were the Newton Gordons, who sent the finest Madeiras to Charleston and Savannah. From 1791 to 1805, their firm was Newton Gordon, Murdock, & Scott. One hundred and ten years ago, they sent five hundred pipes of Madeira in one shipment to Savannah. These wines sent there were the finest Sercials, Buals, and Malmseys. All those wines were known as extra Madeiras. The highest priced wine, a Manigult Heyward wine, I knew forty years ago; it was ninety years old— perfect, full flavored, and of good color and strength.

In Charleston and Savannah from 1780 to 1840, almost every gentleman ordered a pipe of wine from Madeira. I know of a man who has kept this up for half a century.

There is a common prejudice against Malmsey, as being a lady's wine, and sweet; when very old, no Madeira can beat it. I have now in my cellar an "All Saints" wine, named after the famous Savannah Quoit Club, imported in 1791; a perfect wine, of exquisite flavor. My wife's grandfather imported two pipes of Madeira every year, and my father-in-law continued to do this as long as he lived. When he died he had, as I am told, the largest private cellar of Madeira in the United States. All his wines were Newton Gordons. He made the fatal mistake of hermetically sealing them in glass gallon bottles, with ground glass stoppers, keeping them in his cellar; keeping them from light and air, preventing the wine from breathing, as it were. It has taken years for them to recover from this treatment.

Madeira should be kept in the garret. A piece of a corn cob is often a good cork for it. Light and air do not injure it; drawing it off from its lees occasionally, makes it more delicate, but, if done too often, the wine may spoil, as its lees support and nourish it.

The great New York Madeiras, famous when landed and still famous, were "The Marsh and Benson, 1809," "The Coles Madeira," "The Stuyvesant," "The Clark," and "The Eliza." In Philadelphia, "The Butler, 16." In Boston, "The Kirby," the "Amory 1800," and "1811," "The Otis." In Baltimore, "The Marshall," the "Meredith," or "Great Unknown," "The Holmes Demijohn," "The Mob," "The Colt." In Charleston, "The Rutledge," "The Hurricane," "The Earthquake," "The Maid," "The Tradd-street." In Savannah, "The All Saints" (1791), "The Catherine Banks," "The Louisa Cecilia" (1818), "The Rapid" 1817, and "The Widow."

Chapter Twenty-One - Champagnes and Other Wines

The fashionable world here have accepted the *Brût* champagne, and avoid all other kinds; ladies even more than men. But another revolution is to occur in this country in the next five years in the treatment of this wine. We will soon follow the example of our English brethren and never drink it until it is from eight to ten years old.

A year or two ago one of the most fashionable men in London asked me to assist him in ordering a dinner at Delmonico's. When we came to ordering the wines, he exclaimed against the champagne. "What!" said he, "drink a champagne of 1880. Why, it is too absurd!" I told him it was that or nothing, for we were far behind them in England, drinking new champagnes and having no old ones.

The idea is prevalent that champagne will not keep in this climate. After a few years one will always order his supply from abroad yearly, keeping his champagne at his London wine merchant's or at the vineyard. To evidence the improvement in champagne by age, I can only cite that the champagne of

1874 has sold in London at auction for $7 a bottle, and now in Paris and London you pay $8 a bottle for a '74 wine at a restaurant, and $6 for an 1880 wine; at the vineyard itself $45 a dozen, and hard to obtain at this price. If you once drink one of these old champagnes you will never again drink a fresh wine. In England they now drink no Madeira; it is never served. At their dinners they pride themselves on giving 1874 champagne. If they can give this wine, with a Golden Sherry and a fine glass of Port, they are satisfied.

It will be well to remember that champagnes are now known to *connoisseurs* by their vintage. Wines of some vintages do not keep at all. In keeping champagnes, keep only, or order kept for you, the champagnes of the best vintages. Of course, there is much risk in keeping any champagne; but what all strive for, is to possess something that no one else has; that is not purchasable, I mean, in any quantity, and this now is 1874 champagne.

To properly *frappé* champagne, put in the pail small pieces of ice, then a layer of rock salt, alternating these layers until the tub is full. Put the bottle in the tub; be careful to keep the neck of the bottle free from the ice, for the quantity of wine in the neck of the bottle being small, it would be acted upon by the ice first. If possible, turn the bottle every five minutes. In twenty-five minutes from the time it is put in the tub, it should be in perfect condition, and should be served immediately. What I mean by perfect condition is, that when the wine is poured from the bottle, it should contain little flakes of ice; that is a real *frappé*.

It is often a mistake to *frappé*, for it takes both flavor and body from the wine, and none but a very rich, fruity wine should ever be *frappéd*. My theory is that for ordinary cooling of wine, it is not necessary to use salt, unless you are in a hurry. The salt intensifies the cold and makes it act more quickly. You get a speedier result. I should simply use above formula, omitting the salt. Champagne should not be left in a refrigerator for several hours before being served, as it takes away its freshness. In serving it, for one who likes it cold, the wine should be cooled sufficiently to form a bead on the outside of the glass into which it is poured. It is pretty, and the perfection of condition.

In regard to champagne of excellent years, we begin with 1857, as there were no first-rate vintages of this wine between 1846 and 1857. The great years were: 1834, 1846, 1857, 1858, 1861, 1862, 1865, 1868, 1870, 1872, and 1874, the last exceptionally fine and keeping well; 1878, 1880, and 1884, fine wines; 1885 is fair, but not to be classed with the 1884. The Romans noted the years of the celebrated growths of their wines, marked them on their wine vessels, when Rome was a Republic, with the Consul's name, which indicated the vintage. A celebrated vintage was that of the year 632, when Opimius was Consul. It was in high esteem a century afterwards.

In clarets, we also make a mistake; we cling to them when by age they become too thin and watery. One fills up one's wine cellar with claret, and then tenaciously holds it, until it frequently loses the fine characteristics of a first-class wine. The clarets of 1854 promised very great things, but were certainly a failure in Latour, and in some of the other wines of that year; 1857, 1858,

1881, some were good. The claret of 1865 was an extravagant wine, but developed a good deal of acidity, and is not to-day held in very high esteem, but I have tasted some perfect of that year. 1868 promised much, but has not turned out as good as was expected. 1869 sold at very low prices, but has become the best wine of very recent years. 1870 was a very big, full-bodied wine; it is now very good. Of 1871, some of them are excellent (as Haut Brion, Lafitte, Latour). The 1874's were very good, Latour the best; 1875 was very good; 1877, quite good; 1878, very good; 1879, only moderate; 1880, light and delicate, quite good; 1881, big wines, very promising; 1884 promised well, and 1887 promised to be great wines. I do not think it is easy to be certain of Bordeaux wines until they have been in bottles some years. A wine which while in the wood may be excellent, may not ripen the right sort of way in bottles and prove disappointing. Decant all your clarets before serving them, even your *vin ordinaire*. If at a dinner you give both Burgundy and claret, give your finest claret with the roast, your Burgundy with the cheese. Stand up both wines the morning of the dinner, and in decanting, hold the decanter in your left hand, and let the wine first pour against the inside of the neck of the decanter, so as to break its fall. With Burgundy, the Clos Vougeots have run out. The insect has destroyed them. The Chambertins or Romanée Conti, when you give them to those who can appreciate fine wines, have a telling effect.

Table sherries should be decanted and put in the refrigerator one hour before dinner. Personally, as a table sherry I prefer to drink the new, light, delicate sherries, as they come from Spain, directly from the wood, before they are darkened by being kept in glass, and before all the water, that is always in them, has disappeared. This is the taste of the Spanish people themselves. They drink them from the wood.

There is no need of having a large cellar of wine in this country, for we Americans are such Arabs, that we are never contented to stay quietly at home and enjoy our country, and our own perfect climate. No sooner have we built a charming residence, including a wine cellar, than we must needs dash off to Europe, to see what the Prince of Wales is doing, so that literally a New Yorker does not live in his New York residence, at most, more than four or five months in the year. In the other seven or eight, his servants have ample time to leisurely drink up the wine in his cellar, bottle by bottle; therefore, I advise against laying in any large supply of wine. Your wine merchant will always supply you with all wines excepting *old clarets*; these you must have a stock of; and, as servants do not take to claret, you are comparatively safe in hoarding up a good lot of it. Your old champagnes you can order from London, i.e. a winter's supply, every year, for as they say it will not keep in this climate, you must do so to get it of any age. When sherry becomes old and has been kept some time in glass, they then drink it in Spain as a *liqueur*.

If you cannot get hold of the best, the very best and finest old Madeira, give up that wine and take to sherry. I have seen sherry that could not be distinguished from Madeira by experts. Again, I have seen a superb sherry bring a hundred dollars a dozen. The most perfect sherry I ever drank was the "Forsyth sherry," given to Vice-President Forsyth by the Queen of Spain, when he was the American Minister at her Court. I give during dinner a light, delicate, dry Montilla sherry. At dessert, with and after fruit, a fine Amontillado.

Chapter Twenty-Two - Dinners

The Boston fashion adopted here for years, of one's finding, on entering the house in which he was to dine, a small envelope on a silver salver in which was inclosed a card bearing on it the name of the lady assigned to him to take in to dinner, though still in use, is, however, going out of fashion. We are returning to the old habit of assigning the guests in the drawing-room.

In going in to dinner, there is but one rule to be observed. The lady of the house in almost every case goes in last, all her guests preceding her, with this exception, that if the President of the United States dines with you, or Royalty, he takes in the lady of the house, preceding all of the guests. When no ladies are present, the host should ask the most distinguished guest, or the person to whom the dinner is given, to lead the way in to dinner, and he should follow all the guests. The cards on the plates indicate his place to each one. By gesture alone, the host directs his guests to the dining-room, saying aloud to the most distinguished guest, "Will you kindly take the seat on my right?"

The placing of your guests at table requires an intimate knowledge of society. It is only by constant association that you can know who are congenial. If you are assigned to one you are indifferent to, your only hope lies in your next neighbor; and with this hope and fear you enter the dining-room, not knowing who that will be. At the table conversation should be crisp; it is in bad taste to absorb it all. Macaulay, at a dinner, would so monopolize it that the great wit, Sydney Smith, said he did not distinguish between monologue and dialogue.

When the President of the United States goes to a dinner, all the guests must be assembled; they stand in a horseshoe circle around the *salon*; the President enters; when the lady of the house approaches him, he gives her his arm, and they lead the way to the dining-room, the President sitting in the host's place, with his hostess on his right. On arriving at the house where he is to dine, if the guests are not all assembled, he remains in his carriage until he is notified that they are all present. No one can rise to leave the table until the President himself rises. If he happens to be deeply interested in some fair neighbor, and takes no note of time, the patience of the company is sadly tried.

On entering a *salon* and finding yourself surrounded by noted or fashionable people, you are naturally flattered at being included; if the people are unnoted, you are annoyed. The surprise to me is that in this city our cleverest men and politicians do not oftener seek society and become its brilliant ornaments, as in England and on the Continent of Europe. Disraeli, Mr. Gladstone, Lord Palmerston, all were in society and were great diners out. In fact, all the distinguished men of Europe make part and parcel of society; whilst here, they shirk it as if it were beneath their dignity. They should know that there is no power like the social power; it makes and unmakes. The proverb is that, "The way to a man's heart is through the stomach."

Now as to the length of a good dinner. Napoleon the Third insisted on being served in three-quarters of an hour. As usual here we run from one extreme to another. One of our most fashionable women boasted to me that she had dined out the day before, and the time consumed from the hour she left her house, until her return home, was but one hour and forty minutes. This is absurd. A lover of the flesh pots of Egypt grumbled to me that his plate was snatched away from him by the servant before he could half get through the appetizing morsel on it. This state of things has been brought about by stately, handsome dinners, spun out to too great length. One hour and a half at the table is long enough.

A word about the decoration of the table. In this we are now again running from one extreme to the other. A few years ago, the florist took possession of the table, and made a flower garden of it, regardless of cost. Now, at the best dinners, you see perhaps in the centre of the table one handsome basket of flowers; no *bouquets de corsage* or *boutonnières*; the table set with austere simplicity; a few silver dishes with bonbons and *compotiers* of fruit, that is all. Now, nothing decorates a dinner table as flowers do, and of these I think the *Gloire de Paris*roses, the Rothschild rose, and Captain Chrystie's the most effective. A better result is produced by having all of one kind of flower, be it roses, or tulips, or carnations.

It is now the fashion to have the most superb embroidered table-cloths from Paris, in themselves costing nearly a year's income. But it is to be remembered that thirty years ago we imported from England the fashion of placing in the centre of the table a handsome piece of square scarlet satin, on which to place the silver. At the dinner the eye should have a feast as well as the palate. A beautifully laid table is very effective. I have seen Her Majesty's table at Windsor Castle all ready for her. I have heard her footmen, in green and gold, re-echo from hall to kitchen the note that "dinner is served," and then I was told to go; but I saw all I wanted to see. Her six footmen placed their hands on the little velvet Bishop's cap, which covered the lion and the unicorn in frosted gold on the cover of her six *entrée* dishes; as dinner was announced, this velvet cap was removed. The keeper of her jewel room has a large book of lithographs of just the pieces of gold plate that are to decorate Her Majesty's table on different occasions, all regulated by the rank of her guest. Her Majesty, in the time of Prince Albert, dined at 8:15. Her head *chef* informed me then that her real dinner was eaten at 2 P.M., with the Prince of Wales, and it was for this he exercised his talent. At eight and a quarter she took but soup and fish.

It is to be borne in mind that a host or hostess cannot be too courteous or gracious to their guests; and again, that guests in being late at dinner often-times commit a breach of politeness. Apropos of this, whilst in Paris one of our Ministers to the French Court related to me the following anecdote, illustrating true French politeness. His daughter arrived late at the dinner of a high personage. When her father remonstrated, she replied, "Did you not see that one of the family arrived after us?" The next day our Minister heard that the Duchess, with whom he had dined, had sent her daughter out of the room to come in after them, to relieve them of any embarrassment at being late.

Another point has had some discussion. At a large dinner, where the only lady is the hostess, should she rise and receive each guest? This is still a vexed question. Again, at a large dinner of men, is it incumbent on every one present to rise on the entrance of each guest? On one occasion I failed myself to do this, not thinking it necessary. The distinguished man who entered said afterwards that I had "slighted him." It was certainly unintentional. In a small room, if all get up, it must create confusion.

If you intend to decline an invitation to dinner, do so at as early a date as possible. A dinner invitation, once accepted, is a sacred obligation. If you die before the dinner takes place, your executor must attend the dinner. (This is not to be taken literally, but to illustrate the obligation.) The person to whom the dinner is given takes in the hostess, if she is present, going in first with her; that is, if it is only men (no ladies present but the hostess). Should there be ladies, he still takes in the hostess, but then follows all the guests; going in with the hostess after all the guests. The only exception to this rule is where the President of the United States, or Royalty dines with you.

In England, in the note of invitation to dinner, you are never asked *to meet any one* but Royalty. The distinction of rank makes the reason for this obvious. If Royalty dines with you, at the top of the note of invitation, in the left hand corner, it is written: "To meet His Royal Highness," or other Royalty. Our custom is otherwise. It is to invite you to meet Mr. Robinson, or Mrs. Robinson, or Mr. and Mrs. Robinson. This is accepted and approved by all in this country, for in this way you are privileged to invite, at a day's notice, any number of guests; for one sees it is to meet a stranger, temporarily here; a sufficient reason for so short a notice to a large dinner; besides which you have it in your power to pay the stranger or strangers a compliment in a pointed way, by making them or him the honored guest of that dinner.

If you propose accepting, your note of acceptance should be sent the day after the invitation has been received. After dining at a ladies' dinner it is obligatory that you leave your card at the house where you have dined, either the next day or within a day or two. This is called, by the French, a *visite de digestion.* In England, this custom is dying out, for men have not the time to do it.

I would here compare society to a series of intersecting circles; each one is a circle of its own, and they all unite in making what is known as general society. Meeting people at a large ball is no evidence of their being received in the smaller circles. What the French call the *petit comité* of good society is the inmost circle of all, but, naturally, it is confined to a very few. Meeting a person constantly at dinner, at the most exclusive houses, should be sufficient evidence to you that he or she is received everywhere, and if you find people persistently excluded from the best houses at dinners, you may be satisfied that there is some good reason for it.

When you introduce a man into the sanctuary of your own family, it is supposed by a fiction to be the greatest compliment you can pay him; but do not be misled by this, for there is nothing more trying to the guest than to be the one outsider. A friend of mine invariably refuses such invitations. "Why," said he, "my dinner at home is sufficiently good; I am called out with my wife,—both of us compelled to don our best attire, order the carriage, and go to see and be with, whom? A family whose members are not particularly interesting to us." Men with whom you are only on a business footing you should dine at your Club, and not inflict them on your family.

Chapter Twenty-Three – Cooks and Catering

Twenty years ago there were not over three *chefs* in private families in this city. It is now the exception not to find a man of fashion keeping a first-class *chef* or a famous *cordon bleu*. In the last six years Swedish women cooks have come over here, and are excellent, and by some supposed to be better than *chefs*. No woman, in my opinion, can give as finished a dinner as a man. There is always a something in the dinner which has escaped her. It is like German and Italian opera,—there is a finish to the Italian that the Germans can never get. But Swedish cooks deserve special mention; they are really wonderful—cleanliness itself. That is where the French *chef* fails. He must have scullions tracking his very footsteps to keep things clean, while the Swedish woman does her work without making dirt. These women get nearly as large wages as the men,—sixty dollars a month and a scullion maid. What a contrast to living in France! I had the best *chef* in Pau in 1856 for twenty-five dollars, and the scullion received three dollars a month.

The question is often asked, What is the difference in expense to a household between a *chef* or a woman cook? This question is only learned by experience, which teaches me that with a woman, my butcher's bill would be $250 to $275 a month; with a *chef*, $450 to $500. Grocer's bill, with woman cook, say, $75; with a *chef*, $125. This does not include entertaining. For a dinner of twelve or fourteen one's marketing is easily sixty dollars, without the *foie gras* or fruit. An A1 *chef*'s wages is $100 a month; he takes ten per cent. commission on the butcher, grocer, baker, and milkman's bill. If he does not get it directly, he gets it indirectly. In other words, besides his wages, he counts on these commissions. I speak now of the ablest and best; others not quite so capable take five per cent.

Always remember that the Frenchman is a creature of impulses, and works for two things, glory and money. An everyday dinner wearies him, but a dinner *privé*, a special dinner, oh, this calls forth his talent, which shows that the custom some have of calling in and employing a *chef* to cook them a special dinner is correct. If you do not keep a *chef* out of respect for your purse or your health, it is a good plan to know of an "artist" whom you can employ on special occasions, with the express agreement that he submits the list of what he wants, and lets you make the purchases, for these gentry like to make a little *economie*, which always benefits themselves, and such *economie* gives you poor material for him to work upon, instead of good.

How often have I heard a hostess boast, "I never give any attention to the details of my dinner, I simply tell my butler how many people we are to have." In nine cases out of ten this is apparent in the dinner. Madame Rothschild, who has always given the best dinners in Paris, personally supervises everything. The great Duchess of Sutherland, the Queen's friend, when she entertained, inspected every arrangement personally herself. I daily comment to my cook on the performance of the previous day. No one, especially in this country, can accomplish great results without giving time and attention to these details. No French cook will take any interest in his work unless he receives praise and criticism; but above all things, you must know how to criticise. If he finds you are able to appreciate his work when good, and condemn it when bad, he improves, and gives you something of value.

Now let us treat of dinners as given before the introduction of *chefs*, and still preferred by the majority of people.

The best talent with poor material may give a fair dinner, but if the material is poor, the dinner will evidence it. For forty years I have always marketed myself and secured the respect of my butcher, letting him know that I knew as much if not more than he did.

In selecting your shin of beef, remember that a fresh shin is always the best for soup. In choosing fish, look at their gills, which should be a bright red.

See your *filet* cut with the fat well marbled, cut from young beef. Sweetbreads come in pairs; one fine, one inferior. Pay an extra price, and get your butcher to cut them apart and give you only the two large heart breads, leaving to him the two thin throat breads to sell at a reduced price.

In poultry there are two kinds of fat, yellow and white. Fowls fed on rice have white fat; those on corn meal, yellow fat. By the feet of the bird, you can tell its age.

The black and red feathered fowls are always preferred. Never take a gray feathered bird.

Look at the head of the canvasback and the redhead; see them together, and then you will readily see the birds to pick, i.e. the canvasback. Weigh in your hand each snipe or woodcock; the weight will tell you if the bird is fat and plump.

In buying terrapin, look at each one, and see if they are the simon-pure diamond back Chesapeakes.

In choosing your saddle of mutton, take the short-legged ones, the meat coming well down the leg, nearly reaching the foot; a short, thick, stubby little tail; must have the look of the pure Southdown, with black legs and feet.

Of hothouse grapes, I find the large white grapes the best, Muscats of Alexandria.

Parch and grind your coffee the day you drink it. Always buy green coffee.

Never use the small *timbales* of *pâté de foie gras*, generally given one to each guest. Always have an entire *foie gras*, be it large or small, for in this way you are apt to get old *foie gras* thus worked up.

Always buy your *foie gras* from an A1 house, never from the butcher or fruiterer.

I here give as a recollection of the past the

MENU OF AN OLD-FASHIONED SOUTHERN DINNER.

Terrapin Soup and Oyster Soup, or Mock Turtle Soup,
Soft shell or Cylindrical nose Turtle. [A]

Boiled fresh water Trout (known with us at the North
as Chub).

Shad stuffed and baked (we broil it).
Boiled Turkey, Oyster sauce. A roast Peahen.
Boiled Southern Ham.
Escalloped oysters. Maccaroni with cheese. Prawn pie.
Crabs stuffed in shell.
Roast Ducks. A haunch of Venison.

Dessert.
Plum Pudding. Mince Pies. Trifle. Floating Island.
Blanc Mange. Jelly.
Ice Cream.

On repeatedly visiting the West Indies, I found that two of the best Carolina and Georgia dishes, supposed always to have emanated from the African brain, were imported from these islands, and really had not even their origin there, but were brought from Bordeaux to the West Indies, and thence were carried to the South. I refer to the *Crab à la Creole*, and *Les Aubergines farcies à la Bordelaise.*

After the great revolution, when the Africans of Hayti drove from the island their former masters, good French cooking came with them to Baltimore, and other parts of the South. In talking of Southern dishes, I must not forget the Southern barnyard-fed turkey. They were fattened on small rice and were very fine. In discussing Southern dinners, I cannot omit making mention of the old Southern butler, quite an institution; devoted to his master, and taking as much pride in the family as the family took in itself. Among Southern household servants (all colored people), the man bore two names as well as the woman. The one he answered to as servant, the other was his title. Whenever, as a boy, I wanted particularly to gratify my father's old butler, I would give him his title, which was "Major Brown." He was commonly called Nat. I remember, on one occasion, a guest at my father's table asking Major Brown to hand him the rice, whilst he was eating fish. The old gray-haired butler drew himself up with great dignity, and replied, "Massa, we don't eat rice with fish in this house."

Some features of the everyday Southern dinner were *pilau*, i.e. boiled chickens on a bed of rice, with a large piece of bacon between the chickens; "Hoppin John," that is, cowpeas with bacon; okra soup, a staple dish; shrimp and prawn pie; crab salad; pompey head (a stuffed *filet* of veal); roast quail and snipe, and, during the winter, shad daily, boiled, broiled and baked.

As there is reciprocity in everything, if you dine with others, they, in turn, must dine with you. Passing several winters at Nassau, N.P., I dined twice a week, regularly, with the Governor of the Bahamas. I suggested to him the propriety of my giving him a dinner. He smiled, and said:

"My dear fellow, I represent Her Majesty; I cannot, in this town, dine out of my own house."

"Egad!" said I, "then dine with me in the country!"

"That will do," he replied; "but how will you, as a stranger, get up a dinner in this land, where it is a daily struggle to get food?"

"Leave that to me," I said. The Governor's accepting this invitation, recalled a story my father oft related, which caused me some anxiety as to the expense of my undertaking. A distinguished man with whom he was associated at the bar was sent as our Minister to Russia; when he returned home, my father interviewed him as to his Russian experience. He said, that after being repeatedly entertained by the royal family, he felt that it was incumbent on him, in turn, to entertain them himself; so he approached the Emperor's grand Chamberlain and expressed this wish, who at once accepted an invitation to breakfast for the whole Imperial family. "McAllister," he said, "I gave that breakfast; I was charmed with its success, but my dear man, it took my entire fortune to pay for it. I have been a poor man ever since."

Having this party on hand, I went to the *chef* of the hotel, interviewed him, found he had been at one time the head cook of the New York Hotel in this city; so I felt safe in his hands. I went to work and made out a list of all the French dishes that could be successfully rechauffé. Such as *côtelettes de mouton en papillotte, vol au vent à la financière, boudins de volaille à la Richelieu, timbales de riz de veau, et quenelle de volaille*; a boiled Yorkshire ham, easily heated over, to cook which properly it must be simmered from six to seven hours until you can turn the bone; then lay it aside twelve hours to cool; then put it in an oven, and constantly baste it with a pint of cider. It must be served hot, even after being cut. The oftener it is placed in the oven and heated the better it becomes. Thus cooked, they have been by one of my friends hermetically sealed in a tin case and sent to several distinguished men in England, who have found them a great delicacy.

I then hired for the day for $20 a shut-up country place; got plenty of English bunting, quantities of flowers; saw that my champagne was of the best and well *frappéd*; made a speech to the waiters and cook, urging them to show these Britishers what the Yankee could do when put to his stumps; and then with a long cavalcade of cooks, waiters, pots, and pans, heading the procession myself, went off to my orange-grove retreat, some five miles from Nassau, made my men work like beavers, and awaited the arrival of my sixty English guests, who were coming to see the American *fiasco* in the way of a country dinner and *fête*. In they came, and great was their surprise when they beheld a table for sixty people, *pièces montés* of confectionery, flowers, wines all nicely decanted, and a really good French dinner, at once served to them. I only relate this to show that where there is a will there is a way, and that you can so work upon a French cook's vanity that he will, on a spurt like this, outdo himself.

Marvelous to relate, the *chef* positively refused to be recompensed.

"No, sir," he replied; "I am well off; I wish no pay. Monsieur has appreciated my efforts. Monsieur knows when things are well done. He has made a great success. All the darkies on this island could not have cooked that dinner. I am satisfied."

I was so pleased with the fellow, that when he broke down in health he came to me, and I had him as my cook two Newport summers. I kept him alive by giving him old Jamaica rum and milk fresh from the cow, taken before his breakfast,—an old Southern remedy for consumption.

Some of his remarks on Nassau are worthy of repeating. I said to him, "*Chef*, why don't they raise vegetables on this fruitful island? Why bring them all from New York?"

"Monsieur," he replied, "here you sow your seed at night, by midnight it is ripe and fit to cook; by morning it has gone to seed. The same way with sheep. You bring a flock of sheep here, with fine fleeces of wool; in a few months they are goats, and not wool enough on them to plug your ears.

[A] This turtle is only found in the ditches of the rice fields, and is the most valued delicacy of the South. It is too delicate to transport to the North. I have made several attempts to do this, but invariably failed, the turtle dying before it could reach New York. Its shell is gelatinous, all of which is used in the soup. It is only caught in July and August, and even then it is very rare, and brings a high price.

Chapter Twenty-Four - Balls

In 1876, asked by a committee of eighty-two ladies to act as Manager of a ball they were getting up at Chickering Hall, in aid of the "Centennial Union," to be called the "Banner Ball," I accepted their flattering invitation to lead so fair a band of patriots.

On examining the premises, I found that on a new floor they had put a heavy coat of varnish; there was nothing *then* to be done but to sprinkle it thickly with corn meal, and then sweep it off, and renew the dressing from time to time. It is well to say here that if a floor is too slippery (which it often is, if hard wood is used and it is new), there is nothing to be done but to sprinkle it with powdered pumice-stone, sweeping it off before dancing on it; and again, if it is not slippery enough, then, as above, give it repeated doses of corn meal, and the roughest floor is soon put in good condition to dance on.

The opening quadrille of this ball was very effective. We formed in the second story of the Hall. I led the way to the ball-room with the "fairest of the fair," the daughter of one of the most distinguished men in this country (who had not only been Governor of this State, but Secretary of State of the United States). We were surrounded by a noble throng of old New Yorkers, all eager to view the opening quadrille. The ladies were in Colonial costumes, representing Lady Washington and the ladies of her court. As I walked through the crowded rooms, having on my arm one of our brilliant society women, "a flower which was not quite a flower, yet was no more a bud," we met approaching us a lady in indeed gorgeous apparel—so gorgeous, that the lady on my arm at once accosted her with, "Good gracious, my dear Mrs. B——, what have you got on? Let me look at you." Her head was a mass of the most superb ostrich plumes, Prince of Wales feathers, which towered above her, and as she advanced would bend gracefully forward, nodding to you, as it were, to approach and do her honor. Her dress, neck, and shoulders were ablaze with jewels and precious stones, and in her hand she carried an old Spanish fan, such as a queen might envy. The following reply to the query came from this royal dame: "What have I got on? Why, Madame, I had a grandmother!" "Had you, indeed! Then, if that was her garb, she must have been Pocahontas, or the Empress of Morocco!" The war of words beginning to be a little sharp, I pressed on, only to meet another famous lady, whose birthplace was Philadelphia, and who had had no end of grandmothers. She wore a superb dress of scarlet and gold, tight-fitting, such as was worn during the Empire. Another young woman wore her great-grandmother's dress, pink and brown striped brocade, cut like Martha Washington's dress in the Republican Court, in which her great grandmother figured. The wife of a prominent jurist, a remarkably handsome woman, with a grand presence and a noble carriage, representing Lady Washington, wore, to all eyes, the most attractive costume there.

During the winter of 1877, a Southern woman of warm sympathies, great taste, and natural ability, having married a young man of colossal fortune, was urged to take in hand the cause of the wounded Christians in the Russian-Turkish War, and raise funds to send to their relief. To do this, she formed the "Society of the Crescent and the Cross," and a ball was given under her auspices at the Academy of Music, remembered in society as the "Turkish Ball."

This lady did me the honor of making me the Chairman of the Floor Committee of that ball. Consulting with her, we selected the members of the opening quadrille, and took good care to choose the most brilliant women in this city. My partner was one of the greatest belles New York has ever had, a woman of such air and distinction, such beauty of face and charm of manner, as we read of, but rarely see.

Our quadrille, formed on the stage of this large opera house, with the guests of the ball filling the galleries and looking down on it, was no sooner over than I found we were in this dilemma: Our little quadrille was left in full possession of the vast auditorium, and the question was, how to get the people to leave the boxes and come down to us. It was not in any way a full ball, and as the ladies who had danced in the quadrille at once retired to their boxes, they left me, as it were, sole occupant of the dancing floor. However, I rushed around and here and there collected dancing men, and succeeded in getting a respectable number on the floor, and infused spirit into the dancing.

The trouble in such cases is the indisposition of ladies to dance at a public ball, other than in an opening quadrille. The ball, however, went merrily on to a late hour.

A few years later, I was asked to be one of the Floor Committee of the ball to be given to the distinguished French and German officers who came over to join in our celebration of the Centennial of the Battle of Yorktown. This was the invitation:

Office of the French Reception Commission,
Room 7, Fifth Avenue Hotel, New York, 28th October, 1881.
Dear Sir:
The Commissioners appointed by the Governor of the State to extend its courtesies to the guests of the Nation, request that you will act as one of the Floor Committee on the occasion of the Ball to be given at the Metropolitan Casino, on the evening of November 7.
An immediate answer will oblige,

Yours very respectfully,
WILLIAM JAY,
Chairman of the Ball Committee.
To Ward McAllister, Esq.

Experience had taught me never to go on a committee in any social matter unless the committee was formed by myself, or made up of personal friends on whom I could rely, and who would second and support me in my work; for I well knew that it requires hard head-work and hand-work to carry through to success any social project. Sometimes it happens—it has often happened to me—that you have men on a committee with you who are wofully ignorant of the work they have undertaken to superintend, who in one breath tell you "I know nothing about this business," and in the next criticise, discuss, and deluge you with useless and worthless suggestions, and then, when they find they themselves can do nothing turn the whole matter over to you and tell you to "go ahead." You do go ahead and do their work, and then, when they find it is effectual, and they see your efforts will be crowned with success, they quietly come in and appropriate the credit of it.

However, on this occasion I agreed to act, as my duties were confined to forming the opening quadrille, and taking charge of the dancing. Picture to yourself a huge hall, one mass of human beings awaiting the opening of the ball, impatient of delay, anxious to dash off into the waltz, tempted by the inspiriting strains coming from a perfect band of one hundred well-trained musicians. Then, at one end of this vast hall, a stage filled with ladies in brilliant costumes, and foreign officers all in uniform; the Governor of the State, the Mayor of the City, and the chairmen of the various Yorktown committees; then your humble servant as one of the Floor Committee, flitting from one group to another, instructing each of them what they were to do. The position was indeed droll. I stood behind the Governor, who was to all outward appearances conversing with General Boulanger, but was literally squeezing my hand and asking me what he was to do. One distinguished German general promptly said, "I go it blind! I will simply do what the others do." These were the forces I had to marshal and put through a quadrille. I dodged from one to the other and called out the figures, and breathed a sigh of relief when the dance was concluded.

Looking around the galleries and scanning all the distinguished people, my eye lit upon a wonderfully bright and intelligent face. Inwardly I said, "There is a man among men. Who can it be?" My curiosity was so aroused that I went into his box, introduced myself to him as one of the Floor Committee, and said, "I have never seen you before; I know you are a distinguished man. Pray who are you?" Laughingly, he replied, "I am James G. Blaine." "Well," I said, "my instincts have not failed me this time. I have heard and read of you for years. Now I see your genius in your face." Beauty in woman, genius in man, happily I never fail to discover.

The invitation to this ball was as follows:

BALL.

The Commissioners appointed by the State of New York request the honor of your presence to meet the Guests of the Nation at the Metropolitan Casino on the evening of Monday, November 7, at ten o'clock.

New York, 19th of October, 1881.

Some of the distinguished guests of the Nation were M. Max Outrey, Ministre Plenipotentiare de la France aux Etats-Unis, M. le Marquis de Rochambeau, General Boulanger, le Comte de Beaumont, and le Comte de Corcelle, representing the Lafayettes, and Colonel A. von Steuben, representing the family of Major-General von Steuben.

Chapter Twenty-Five – Famous Newport Balls

The next great event in the fashionable world was a Newport ball. A lady who had married a man of cultivation and taste, a member of one of New York's oldest families, who had inherited from her father an enormous fortune, was at once seized with the ambition to take and hold a brilliant social position, to gratify which she built one of the handsomest houses in this city, importing interiors from Europe for it, and such old Spanish tapestries as had never before been introduced into New York; after which she went to Newport, and bought a beautiful villa on Bellevue Avenue, and there gave, in the grounds of that villa, the handsomest ball that had ever been given there. The villa itself was only used to receive and sup the guests in, for a huge tent, capable of holding fifteen hundred people, had been spread over the entire villa grounds, and in it was built a platform for dancing. The approaches to this tent were admirably designed, and produced a great effect. On entering the villa itself, you were received by the hostess, and then directed by liveried servants to the two improvised *salons* of the tent. The one you first entered was the Japanese room, adorned by every conceivable kind of old Japanese objects of art, couches, hangings of embroideries, cunning cane houses, all illuminated with Japanese lanterns, and the ceiling canopied with Japanese stuffs, producing, with its soft reddish light, a charming effect; then, behind tables scattered in different parts of the room, stood Japanese boys in costume, serving fragrant tea. Every possible couch, lounge, and easy-chair was there to invite you to sit and indulge yourself in ease and repose.

Leaving this ante-room, you entered still another *salon*, adorned with modern and Parisian furniture, but furnished with cunningly devised corners and nooks for "flirtation couples"; and from this you were ushered into the gorgeous ball-room itself,—an immense open tent, whose ceiling and sides were composed of broad stripes of white and scarlet bunting; then, for the first time at a ball in this country, the electric light was introduced, with brilliant effect. Two grottos of immense blocks of ice stood on either side of the ball-room, and a powerful jet of light was thrown through each of them, causing the ice to resemble the prisms of an illuminated cavern, and fairly to dazzle one with their coloring. Then as the blocks of ice would melt, they would tumble over each other in charming glacier-like confusion, giving you winter in the lap of summer; for every species of plant stood around this immense floor, as a flowering border, creeping quite up to these little improvised glaciers. The light was thrown and spread by these two powerful jets, sufficiently strong to give a brilliant illumination to the ball-room. The only criticism possible was, that it made deep shadows.

All Newport was present to give brilliancy to the scene. Everything was to be European, so one supped at small tables as at a ball in Paris, all through the night. Supper was ready at the opening of the ball, and also as complete and as well served at the finish, by daylight. Newport had never seen before, and has never since seen, anything as dazzling and brilliant, as well conceived, and as well carried out, in every detail.

Desirous of obtaining an office from the administration of President Arthur, I went to Washington with letters to the President and his Attorney-General. On my arrival, depositing my luggage in my room at Willard's, I descended to the modest little barber-shop of that hotel, and there, in the hands of a colored barber, I saw our distinguished Secretary of State, the Hon. Frederick T. Frelinghuysen, who, on catching sight of me, exclaimed:

"Halloa, my friend! what brings you here?" He had for years been my lawyer in New Jersey.

I replied: "I want an office."

"Well, what office?"

I told him what I wanted.

"I hope you do not expect me to get it for you!" he exclaimed.

"Not exactly," I answered. "My man is the Attorney-General, and I want you to tell me where I can find him."

"Find him! why, that's easy enough; there is not another such man in Washington. Where do you dine?"

"Here in this house, at seven."

"He dines here at the same hour. All you have to do is to look about you then, and when you see an old-fashioned, courtly gentleman of the Benjamin Franklin style, you will see Brewster," said Mr. Frelinghuysen.

While quietly taking my soup, I saw an apparition! In walked a stately, handsome woman, by her side an old-fashioned, courtly gentleman, in a black velvet sack coat, ruffled shirt, and ruffled wristbands, accompanied by a small boy, evidently their son. "There he is," I said to myself. Now, I make it a rule never to disturb any one until they have taken off the edge of their appetite. I stealthily viewed the man on whom my hopes hinged. Remarkable to look at he was. A thoroughly well-dressed man, with the unmistakable air of a gentleman and a man of culture. As he spoke he gesticulated, and even with his family, he seemingly kept up the liveliest of conversations. No sooner had he reached his coffee, than I reached him. In five minutes I was as much at home with him as if I had known him for five years.

"Well, my dear sir," he said, "what made you go first to Frelinghuysen? Why did you not come at once to me? I know all about you; my friends are your friends. I know what you want. The office you wish, I will see that you get. Our good President will sanction what I do. The office is yours. Say no more about it." From that hour this glorious old man and myself were sworn friends; I was here simply carrying out the axiom to keep one's friendships in repair; and, as he had done so much for me, I resolved, in turn, to do all I could for him, and I know I made the evening of his life, at least, one of pleasurable and quiet enjoyment. He came to me that summer at Newport, and the life he there led among fashionable people seemed to be a new awakening to him of cultivated and refined enjoyment. He found himself among people there who appreciated his well-stored mind and his great learning. He was the brightest and best conversationalist I have ever met with. His memory was marvelous; every little incident of everyday life would bring forth some poetical illustrations from his mental storehouse.

At a large dinner I gave him, to which I had invited General Hancock and one of the Judges of the Supreme Court of the United States, the question of precedence presented itself. I sent in the Judge before the General, and being criticised for this, I appealed to the General himself. "In Washington," he said, "I have been sent in to dinner on many occasions before our Supreme Court Judges, and again on other occasions they have preceded me. There is no fixed rule; but I am inclined to think I have precedence."

During this summer, a young friend of mine was so charmed with the Attorney-General, that he advised with me about giving him an exceptionally handsome entertainment. This idea took shape the following winter, when he came and asked me to assist him in getting up for him a superb banquet at Delmonico's. He wanted the brilliant people of society to be invited to it, and no pains or expense to be spared to make it the affair of the winter. I felt that our distinguished citizen, the ex-Secretary of State and ex-Governor, who had so long held political as well as social power, and his wife, should be asked to preside over it, and thus expressed myself to him, and was requested to ask them to do so. I presented myself to this most affable and courtly lady in her sunshiny drawing-room on Second Avenue, and proffered my request. She graciously accepted the invitation, saying she well knew the gentleman and his family as old New Yorkers; and to preside over a dinner given to her old friend, Mr. Brewster, would really give her the greatest pleasure.

Great care was taken in the selection of the guests. New York sent to this feast the brilliant men and women of that day, and the feast was worthy of them. The "I" table (shape of letter I) was literally a garden of superb roses; a border of heartsease, the width of one's hand, encircled it, and was most artistic. Delmonico's ball-room, where we dined, had never been so elaborately decorated. The mural decorations were superb; placques of lilies of the valley, of tulips, and of azaleas adorned the walls; and the dinner itself was pronounced the best effort of Delmonico's *chefs*. What added much to the general effect was on leaving the table for a short half-hour to find the same dining-room, in that short space of time, converted into a brilliant ball-room, all full of the guests of the Patriarchs, and a ball under full headway.

Chapter Twenty-Six – An Era of Extravagance

We here reach a period when New York society turned over a new leaf. Up to this time, for one to be worth a million of dollars was to be rated as a man of fortune, but now, bygones must be bygones. New York's ideas as to values, when fortune was named, leaped boldly up to ten millions, fifty millions, one hundred millions, and the necessities and luxuries followed suit. One was no longer content with a dinner of a dozen or more, to be served by a couple of servants. Fashion demanded that you be received in the hall of the house in which you were to dine, by from five to six servants, who, with the butler, were to serve the repast. The butler, on such occasions, to do alone the head-work, and under him he had these men in livery to serve the dinner, he to guide and direct them. Soft strains of music were introduced between the courses, and in some houses gold replaced silver in the way of plate, and everything that skill and art could suggest was added to make the dinners not a vulgar display, but a great gastronomic effort, evidencing the possession by the host of both money and taste.

The butler from getting a salary of $40 a month received then from $60 to $75 a month. The second man jumped up from $20 to $35 and $40, and the extra men, at the dinner of a dozen people or more, would cost $24. Then the orchids, being the most costly of all flowers, were introduced in profusion. The canvasback, that we could buy at $2.50 a pair, went up to $8 a pair; the terrapin were $4 apiece. Our forefathers would have been staggered at the cost of the hospitality of these days.

Lady Mandeville came over to us at this epoch, and at once a superb fancy ball was announced by one of our fashionable rich men. Every artist in the city was set to work to design novel costumes—to produce something in the way of a fancy dress that would make its wearer live ever after in history. Determining not to be outdone, I went to a fair dowager, who was up in all things; asked for and followed her advice. "Mapleson is your man. Put yourself in his hands," said she; so off I went to him, and there I found myself, not only in his hands, but under the inspection of a fine pair of female eyes, who sat by his side and essayed to prompt him as to what my dress should be.

"Why, man alive!" said she, "don't you see he is a Huguenot all over, an admirer of our sex. Put him in the guise of some woman's lover."

"By Jove, you are right, my fair songster!" said Mapleson. "I'll make him the lover of Marguerite de Valois, who was guillotined at thirty-six because he loved 'not wisely, but too well.' Pray, what is your age?"

"Young enough, my dear sir, to suit your purpose. Go ahead, and make of me what you will," I replied.

"Have you a good pair of legs?"

"Aye, that I have! But at times they are a little groggy. Covering they must have."

"Ah, my boy, we will fix you. Buckskin will do your business. With tights of white chamois and silk hose, you can defy cold." So into the business I went; and when my good friend the Attorney-General came into my room, and saw two sturdy fellows on either side of me holding up a pair of leather trunks, I on a step-ladder, one mass of powder, descending into them, an operation consuming an hour, he exclaimed, "Why, my good sir, your pride should be in your legs, not your head!"

"At present," I said, "it certainly is."

The six quadrilles were really the event of the ball, consisting of "The Hobby-horse Quadrille," the men who danced in it being dressed in "pink," and the ladies wearing red hunting-coats and white satin skirts, all of the period of Louis XIV. In the "Mother Goose Quadrille" were "Jack and Jill," "Little Red Riding-Hood," "Bo-Peep," "Goody Two-Shoes," "Mary, Mary, Quite Contrary," and "My Pretty Maid." The "Opera Bouffe Quadrille" was most successful; but of all of them, "The Star Quadrille," containing the youth and beauty of the city, was the most brilliant. The ladies in it were arrayed as twin stars, in four different colors, yellow, blue, mauve, and white. Above the forehead of each lady, in her hair, was worn an electric light, giving a fairy and elf-like appearance to each of them. "The Dresden Quadrille," in which the ladies wore white satin, with powdered hair, and the gentlemen white satin knee breeches and powdered wigs, with the Dresden mark, crossed swords, on each of them, was effective. The hostess appeared as a Venetian Princess, with a superb jeweled peacock in her hair. The host was the Duke de Guise for that evening. The host's eldest brother wore a costume of Louis XVI. His wife appeared as "The Electric Light," in white satin, trimmed with diamonds, and her head one blaze of diamonds. The most remarkable costume, and one spoken of to this day, was that of a cat; the dress being of cats' tails and white cats' heads, and a bell with "Puss" on it in large letters. A distinguished beauty, dressed as a Phœnix, adorned with diamonds and rubies, was superb, and the Capuchin Monk, with hood and sandals, inimitable; but to name the most striking would be to name all.

The great social revolution that had occurred in New York this winter, like most revolutionary waves, reached Newport. Our distinguished New York journalist then made Newport his summer home, buying the fine granite house that for years had been first known as "The Middleton Mansion," afterwards the "Sidney Brooks residence," and filling it with distinguished Europeans. His activity and energy gave new life to the place.

One fine summer morning, one of his guests, an officer in the English army, a bright spirit and admirable horseman, riding on his polo pony up to the Newport Reading-room, where all the fossils of the place, the nobs, and the swells daily gossiped, he was challenged to ride the pony into the hall of this revered old club, and being bantered to do it, he actually did ride the pony across the narrow piazza, and into the hall of the club itself. This was enough to set Newport agog. What sacrilege! an Englishman to ride in upon us, not respecting the sanctity of the place! It aroused the old patriots, who were members of that Institution, with the spirit of '76, and a summary note was sent to the great journalist, withdrawing the invitation the club had previously given his guest. The latter, in turn, felt aggrieved, and retaliated with this result: Building for Newport a superb Casino, embracing a club, a ball-room, and a restaurant, opposite his own residence. All this evidencing that agitation of any kind is as beneficial in social circles, as to the atmosphere we breathe.

Then our journalist conceived and gave a handsome domino ball. All the ladies in domino, much after the pattern of the one previously given by the Duchess de Dino, and in many respects resembling it, having a huge tent spread behind the house, and all the rooms on the first floor converted into a series of charming supper-rooms, each table decorated most elaborately with beautiful flowers; as handsome a ball as one could give. I took the wife of the Attorney-General to it in domino, who, after her life in Washington, was amazed at the beauty of the scene. The grounds, which were very handsome, were all, even the plants themselves, illuminated with electric lights—that is, streams of electric light were cunningly thrown under the plants, giving an illumination *à giorno*, and producing the most beautiful effect.

At this ball there appeared a Blue Domino that set all the men wild. Coming to the ball in her own carriage (her servants she felt she could trust not to betray her) she dashed into the merry throng, and gliding from one to the other whispered airy nothings into men's ears. But they contained enough to excite the most intense curiosity as to who she was. She was the belle of the evening; she became bold and daring at times, attacking men of and about the inmost secrets of their hearts, so as to alarm them, and when she had worked them all up to a fever heat, she came to me to take her to the door that she might make good her escape. A dozen men barricaded the way, but with the rapidity of a deer she dashed through them, reached the sidewalk, and her footman literally threw her into the carriage. Her coachman, well drilled, dashed off at a furious rate, and to this day no one has ever found out who the fair creature was.

The next social event after this grand ball was a large breakfast the great journalist gave for the Duke of Beaufort, at Southwick's Grove. We all sat at tables under the trees, and we had what the French so aptly term a *déjeuner dinatoire*. At it the Duke was most eloquent in his wonderful description of a fishing exploit he had had that morning; rising at 2 A.M., and driving to "Black Rock," he groped his way to the farthest point, and had the satisfaction of hooking an enormous bass. In his own words, "As I saw him on the crest of the wave, I knew I had him, and then my sport began."

Hearing that President Arthur would visit Newport, as I felt greatly in his debt I resolved to do my share in making his visit pleasant and agreeable. He was to be the guest of Governor Morgan, whom I at once buttonholed and to him gave the above views. I found, like all these great political magnates, that he preferred to have the President to himself, and rather threw cold water on my attempting anything in my humble way at entertaining him. "Why, my dear sir," he replied, "the President will not go to one of your country picnics. It is preposterous to think of getting up such a rural thing for him. I shall, of course, dine him and give him a fête, and have already sent to New York for my Madeira."

"Sent for your Madeira!" I exclaimed. "Why, my dear Governor, it will not be fit to drink when it reaches you."

"Why not?" he asked.

"Because it will be so shaken up, it will be like tasting bad drugs. Madeira of any age, if once moved, cannot be tasted until it has had at least a month's repose. President Arthur is a good judge of Madeira, and he would not drink your wine."

"Well, what am I to do?" said he.

"Why, my dear Governor, I will myself carry to your house for him a couple of bottles of my very best Madeira." This I did, sitting in the middle of the carriage, one bottle in each hand (it having been first carefully decanted), and into the Governor's parlor I was ushered, and then placed my offering before the President, telling him that I well knew he loved women, as well as song and wine; prayed him to honor me with his presence at a Newport picnic, promising to cull a bouquet of such exotics as are only grown in a Newport hothouse. The invitation he at once accepted, much, I thought, to the chagrin of the Governor, who, accompanying me to his front door, said:

"My dear sir, one must remember that he is the President of the United States, ruling over sixty millions of people. He is here as my guest, and now to go off and dine on Sunday with a leader of fashion, and then to follow this up by attending one of your open-air lunches, seems to me not right." (I must here say in his defense, that the Governor had never been to one of my "open-air lunches," and knew not of what he spoke.)

I then resolved to make this picnic worthy of our great ruler, and at once invited to it a beautiful woman, one who might have been selected for a Madonna. This is the first time I have made mention of her; she possessed that richness of nature you only see in Southern climes; one of the most beautiful women in America. She promised to go to this country party, and bring her court with her.

I selected the loveliest spot on Newport Island, known as "The Balch Place," near "The Paradise and Purgatory Rocks," for this fête. The Atlantic Ocean, calm and unruffled, lay before us; all the noise it made was the gentle ripple of the waves as they kissed the rocky shore. Giving the President our great beauty, he led the way to the collation, partaken of at little tables under the sparse trees that the rough winter barely permitted to live, and then we had a merry dance on the green, on an excellent platform fringed with plants.

At a subsequent breakfast, I was intensely gratified to have the President say to me, before the whole company, "McAllister, you did indeed redeem your promise. The beauty of the women at your picnic, the beauty of the place, and its admirable arrangement—made it the pleasantest party I have had at Newport,"—and this was said before my friend the Governor. Grand, elaborate entertainments are ofttimes not as enjoyable as country frolics.

Chapter Twenty-Seven - Washington Dinners and New York Balls

The following winter my friend Attorney-General Brewster invited me to Washington to pass a fortnight with him, and I then got a glimpse of modern life in that city. I enjoyed my visit, but found the people slower of action than we are in New York; for instance, it took my kind host fully a week to consider over and map out a dinner for me. Then, just as I was leaving, the President asked me to dine with him. I was informed that it was imperative that I should cancel other engagements and remain over to accept his invitation.

The arrangement of the guests at this dinner was to me amusing. Reaching the White House, I was separated from the ladies I brought, and could not in any way find them again to enter the drawing-room with them, but was ushered into it from a side door, and there joined the gentlemen, who stood in line on one side of the room, while from an opposite door the ladies entered the same room, and formed in line, as it were, opposite the men. When all were assembled, the President himself entered, bowed to his guests, and offered his arm to one of the ladies, and led the way in to dinner.

The view from the dining-room into the conservatories, displaying the finest collection of white azaleas I have ever seen, was most effective. The dinner was good, and well served; the President most gracious. Turning to me, he said, "Why, your friend Winthrop is not himself to-day. What is the matter with him?" I replied, "My dear Mr. President, he has been up to the Capitol, and seen his ancestor in white marble, and found his nose was shockingly dirty. This annoyed and mortified him." The President replied, "Really, well, this is too bad! This matter shall at once have my attention. That nose shall be wiped to-morrow!"

The winters of 1884 and 1885 will long be remembered by New York society people, for three of the largest, handsomest, and most successful balls ever given in this city have made them memorable. The heir to probably the largest fortune ever left to one man in this country, then threw open the doors of his palatial residence and generously invited all who were in any way entitled to an invitation, to come and view his superb house, and join in the dance which was to inaugurate its completion.

As I went up the beautiful stairs and passed along the gallery, looking down on a hall such as few palaces contain, with a long train of handsomely dressed women passing me on their way down to the reception room, it put me in mind of a scene I well remembered at the Hôtel de Ville, in Paris, at a ball given by the Emperor Napoleon III. to the King of Sardinia. It looked royal, and was most impressive. Our host stood in the centre of his hall, giving to all a warm welcome. Passing him we entered his *grand salon*, where his wife received us. The room itself, Oriental, and as Eastern and luxurious in its own peculiar style as one could create it. From this *salon*, we entered a novel Japanese room, and then the fine dining-room of the house, with its marvelous ceiling, painted by one of the best modern French artists. The picture galleries were the ball and supper rooms. The cotillion was danced in the farthest of the two galleries, the ladies seated in double and triple lines on improvised seats, as if they were sitting on a long extended dais all around the room. The effect was dazzling and brilliant. All supped well, for when supper was announced little tables were placed like magic through the rooms; and New Yorkers had what they well knew how to appreciate—an elaborate, well-served repast; champagne in abundance, and of the best, and in perfect condition. In my opinion, it was one of the handsomest, most profuse, liberal, and brilliant balls ever given in this country.

The next great flutter in New York's fashionable world was the announcement of a grand entertainment to be given, embracing all the features of a London ball, which, though a novelty here, had for years been done in London; that was to build an addition to one's house, to be used but for one night, and to be made large enough to comfortably hold, with the house, one thousand or twelve hundred people. There was plenty of energy and talent to carry this out, and reproduce here what Londoners have always been so proud of—their ability to double the capacity of their city houses by utilizing their yards, covering them with a temporary structure, to be used as a supper or ball room. A young man of an old Long Island family had married a beautiful girl, a young woman such as Walter Scott would have taken to impersonate his character of Amy Robsart, who, besides this natural and *naïve* style of beauty, possessed great administrative ability, and withal much taste, a great amount of energy, and a fortune large enough to carry through any enterprise she conceived. Both of them were devoted to society, and to each other. Passing their summers abroad, and seeing what vast conceptions society there undertook, and successfully carried out, they resolved to repeat here what they had seen on the other side of the water. In Marcotte they had a great ally, a man of wonderful taste and ability; planning out the work themselves, with his skillful hand to execute it, they certainly built up in a night, as it were, a superb banqueting hall, complete and elaborately finished as if a part of the house itself; a solid structure, with no appearance of its being temporary or run up for the occasion. Throwing two houses into one, and descending from them into this vast banqueting hall by a wide flight of stairs, you had, to all appearances, a grand palatial residence, whose rooms the largest crowd could roam through with freedom and perfect comfort. The houses themselves were so handsomely decorated in the period of Louis XIV., that it required cultivated taste to add floral decorations to such rooms; but it was done, and admirably done, and was a remarkable feature of this superb ball. Garlands of the delicate *La France* roses were festooned on the walls, and over and around the doors and windows, producing a charming effect. There were two cotillions danced in separate rooms. The approach from the street to the houses was admirable; the pavement was inclosed the entire length of both, carpeted, and brilliantly lighted with innumerable jets of gas—a ball long to be remembered!

What then was there left for one to do in the way of entertaining to give society anything new and novel? This duty was then imposed on me. These pages bear evidence that I am blessed with memory, but imagination was then what I required to conceive and carry out some new enterprise in the way of a subscription New Year's ball, to surpass anything I had ever before given.

The most difficult rooms to decorate are those at Delmonico's; but this establishment is unequaled in London or Paris in that it gives under its roof incomparable balls, banquets, and dinners. So we resolved that talent, taste, and money should be expended in an effort to design and give there a superb ball. The house had the advantage of having a large square room, all that was required for a dance of three to four hundred people. On this occasion we were to have seven hundred, and for so large a number we had to provide two *salles de danse*. The upper supper room we turned into a conservatory. Its ceilings were low, but covering them with creeping plants, making around the entire room a dado of banks of flowers and the walls themselves decorated with plaques of roses, introducing the electric light and throwing its jets through all the foliage, we had an improvised bower of flowers and plants that tempted all to wander through, if not to linger in it in admiration of the artistic skill which produced such a result. One room we converted, with Vantine's assistance, into a perfect Japanese interior. Once in it, we felt transported to that country. Here were served tea and Japanese confections, and over all shone the electric light with charming effect. The *salon* known as the Red Room had its walls decorated with sheaves of wheat, in which nestled bunches of *Marechale Neil* roses, the background of scarlet bringing these decorations out strikingly. This, with a new floor, was converted into a *salle de danse*. The large hall into which all these rooms opened was superb, for on all sides of it, from floor to ceiling, were hung the finest Gobelin tapestries of fabulous value. To obtain their use we had to telegraph to Paris, and were required to insure them for a large sum. Servants in light plush livery, pumps, and silk stockings, with powdered hair, stood on either side to direct the guests. Having the whole house, we supped in both restaurant and café, and as we had given an unlimited order had an elaborate and exquisite supper.

For a small ball of seven hundred people, I have always felt, and still feel, that this New Year's Ball, as given at Delmonico's, was in every sense of the word the handsomest, most complete, and most successful thing of the kind that I have ever attempted in New York City, and I find I am not alone in this opinion. It was as much a feast for the eye as the elaborate supper was for the palate, being complete in every detail, luxurious in adornment, as to its rooms—and epicurean in its feasting.

New York society had now become so large that it seemed necessary to solve at once what, to us, has long been a problem, i.e. where we could bring general society together in one large dancing-room; for though you may have a dozen rooms thrown open, you will always find that all rush to the room where there is dancing. Where then could we get a room where all could at one and the same time be on the floor? It occurred to me that the Metropolitan Opera House had, in its stage and auditorium, such a room, and if we could only divest it of its characteristics, it would be what we wanted.

Satisfying ourselves that we could accomplish this, we formed a Committee of Three and entered on this new enterprise. Artists, who have with ability painted small pictures, may venture on larger canvas. We had succeeded in giving balls of seven hundred and four hundred people. Why not have a similar success on a larger scale? Had our ideas been properly carried out, this ball would have been twice the success it was. The defects were evident, but when seen it was too late to remedy them. The artificial ceiling, cleverly planned to shut out the galleries, was not completed, the electric lights were not shaded as they should have been, and the music stands, ordered by the authorities to be elevated, were unsightly, and marred the brilliant effect we had studied to produce. All else received more praise than criticism.

The four most striking points of this ball were, first, the reception of over twelve hundred people as at a private house by three of our most brilliant and accomplished society ladies; again, what may be termed the *Quadrille d'Honneur* of that ball, which was the different sets of the Sir Roger de Coverly, danced by the most distinguished ladies of this city, the "nobs" and the "swells" on this occasion uniting; the supping of over twelve hundred people at one time at small tables, and the cotillion ably led by one of our distinguished State Senators, a man in himself representing family, wealth, and political position.

The Sir Roger de Coverly was danced in the auditorium and on the stage, and before its completion a blast from the *cornet à piston* was sounded by direction of the Management, when at once the three members of the Executive Committee sought the three lady patronesses who had so graciously received for them the guests of this large ball, and had the honor of taking them in to supper. A special table in the centre of the supper room, elaborately decorated with flowers, was arranged for them, and the handsome and courteous gentleman who so royally dispenses hospitality both at his house in town and at his ocean villa in Newport (the handsomest country residence in the United States), at once sought one of America's loveliest, most beautiful, and most graceful daughters, a charming representative of an old Colonial family, and doubly a New Yorker, representing the historic families of Livingston and Ludlow. Another member of the Committee, a descendant of one of our oldest families, whose ancestor was a distinguished General in the Revolution, had the fortune to have on his arm a most superbly dressed woman, whose tiara of diamonds could well have graced a Queen's brow—whose beauty I have before alluded to when comparing her to Amy Robsart. I had the honor of leading the way with our leader of society, whom Worth had adorned with a robe of such magnificence that it attracted and held the attention of the whole assembly. Her jewels were resplendent—in themselves a King's ransom; and placing her on my right, at the supper table, I had on my left the beautiful woman who had won the hearts of the American nation.

Before leaving this ball, I must mete out due praise to the man who could so successfully care for so large a number of people at supper at one time, and give credit to the good and effective work done by the three hundred well-trained, liveried servants scattered through the house, understanding their work and performing it admirably. This ball was given as a New Year's Ball on the 2d of January, 1890.

And now, in concluding this book, I beg to say that I have simply discussed society as I have found it, and only such entertainments of which I have been part and parcel.